INSIDE THE
MIND OF GOD

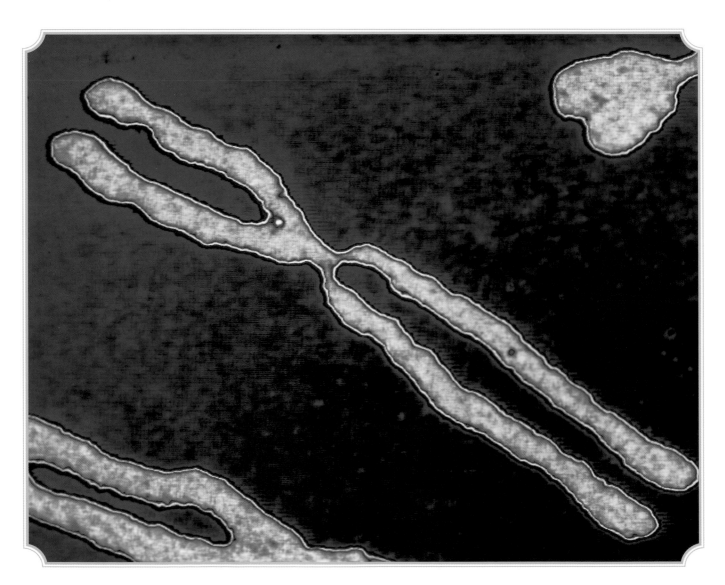

You can observe a lot just by watching.—Yogi Berra

INSIDE THE MIND OF GOD

Images and Words of Inner Space

Introduction by Sharon Begley

Edited by Michael Reagan

TEMPLETON FOUNDATION PRESS

PHILADELPHIA AND LONDON

Inside the Mind of God

First edition
Published by Templeton Foundation Press
Five Radnor Corporate Center, Suite 120
Radnor, Pennsylvania 19087

www.templetonpress.org

Library of Congress Cataloging-in-Publication Data
Inside the mind of God : images and words of inner space / introduction by
Sharon Begley ; edited by Michael Reagan.
    p.   cm.
    ISBN 1-890151-97-1 (alk. paper)
    1. Religion and science. 2. Creation. I. Reagan, Michael, 1945-

BL240.3 .I57 2002
215.7—dc21   2002072235

Printed in Italy

02 03 04 05 06 07   10 9 8 7 6 5 4 3 2 1

Produced by Lionheart Books, Ltd.
5105 Peachtree Industrial Boulevard
Atlanta, Georgia 30341

Design: Carley Wilson Brown & Michael Reagan
Research: Susan Ehring

Cover Image: *Tensor Map of the Brain*, Laboratory of Neuro Imaging, Dr. Arthur W. Toga, Director
Frontispiece: *X Chromosome*, Alfred Pasieka/SPL/Photo Researchers, Inc.
Back Cover Image: Two T-lymphocytes, ©Stem Jems/Photo Researchers

Photography Credits

Introduction

by Sharon Begley

The Reverend William Paley (1743–1805) was born more than two centuries before the invention of the scanning electron microscope, and so was never treated to the dazzling images of flagellum-wagging sperm swarming over an egg like ants over a fallen ice-cream cone at a summer picnic. The Reverend James McCosh (1811–1894) was born at least a century too early to have access to a transmission electron microscope, and so he never saw the exquisite architecture of a synapse, the junction where two neurons meet. He missed out on seeing the intricate design that allows information encoded in electrical signals to reach the end of one neuron and stimulate the release of versatile chemicals called neurotransmitters, which diffuse across the synaptic gap to trigger a new electric impulse in the receiving neuron—and thus the physical basis for thoughts and feelings, memories and dreams. But both McCosh, an American theologian and the eleventh president of Princeton University, and Paley, an English theologian who exemplified the British tradition in natural

theology, were awestruck by what they saw with no more than their naked eyes.

And from that awe grew a strand in philosophy that continues to this day: using the wondrously complex machinery that constitutes living things to infer not merely the existence but even the attributes of the mind of God.

Paley's *Natural Theology*, published in 1802, was one of the most influential books of its century. Natural theology in general refers to the belief that the harmony and precise workings of nature testify to the existence of a Creator and, more than that, mirror his benevolence and intelligence. By studying the creation, natural theology holds, one may infer not only the existence of a Creator but also His characteristics, above all His goodness. Paley's version of natural theology focused less on the overall beauty and harmony of nature and more on the remarkable fit between the design of living things and their functions, what he called the "argument from design." In his most famous parable, Paley describes taking a walk on the heath. If you come upon a stone during your walk, he wrote, you can properly chalk it up to a natural occurrence. Not so if you happen upon a watch during your perambulations. A timepiece is too complex to be natural, Paley argued; it shows clear evidence of design, and must therefore have both a designer and a maker. Just as a telescope is designed and has a human designer, so the marvelous design of the eye implies a divine designer; just as a float is designed and has a human designer, so the wonderful swimbladder of a fish has design and must therefore have a divine designer. "Contrivance must have had a contriver, design, a designer," he wrote.

To a theologian of the early 19th century, of course, that designer was the Christian God. "Every manifestation of design, which existed in the watch, exists in the works of nature," Paley went on. He and his followers had no need to appeal to the exquisitely formed neuron to argue that something so perfectly fitted to its function must have been "contrived," or designed. The plain old mole did just fine. How did it come to be, Paley asked, that the common mole has both "a small sunk eye" and a "shovel palmated foot," the better to burrow and live underground? Surely a palmated foot could develop on an animal with bulging eyes; surely small eyes could characterize an animal with any other form of foot. Yet here are these two adaptations joined in a single animal, perfectly suiting it to its niche in nature. "What was it therefore that which brought them together in the mole?" Paley asked his readers. "That which brought together the barrel, the chain, and the fusee, in a watch," he

answered himself: "design, and design, in both cases, inferred, from the relation which the parts bear to one another in the prosecution of a common purpose."

Paley's arguments were enormously appealing to the English intelligentsia of the time. One comment will suffice. "I do not think I hardly ever admired a book more than Paley's *Natural Theology*," Charles Darwin wrote to a neighbor in November 1859, just a week before the publication of his *On the Origin of Species by Means of Natural Selection*. For many—though perhaps not for Darwin—one of the appeals of Paley's thesis was that it offered reassurance of God's benevolence and care. "The hinges in the wings of an earwig, and the joints of its antennae, are as highly wrought as if the Creator had had nothing else to finish," Paley wrote. "We see no signs of diminution of care by multiplication of objects, or of distraction of thought by variety. We have no reason to fear, therefore, our being forgotten, or overlooked, or neglected," for surely if God could take pains to construct an earwig's wing joints just so, then, too, would he not neglect his finest creations.

In his 1869 book, *Typical Forms and Species Ends in Creation*, McCosh presented the American perspective on all this. He argued that two principles find expression in all living beings: "the principle of order" and "the principle of special adaptation." Both stand in mute testimony to the benevolence and sense of order characteristic of God. By "order,"

McCosh explained, he meant "a general plan, pattern, or type, to which every given object is made to conform"—in other words, the beauty and symmetry omnipresent in living things. By "special adaptation," he wrote, he meant a "particular end, by which each object, while constructed after a general model is, at the same time, accommodated to the situation which it has to occupy"—that is, the exquisite matching of form to function, by which precisely those molecular and cellular structures necessary for a purpose arise everywhere in the natural world. He knew nothing of DNA, of course, but surely he would have been impressed by how the helical, paired-nucleotide structure unzips to form a template able to form an exact replica of itself, the basis of all growth and reproduction.

In a similar vein, the natural historian Louis Agassiz (1807–1873) believed that by studying the works of nature humans could intuit not merely God's existence but also his thoughts and intentions. To that end, he concluded, taxonomy—the classification of, and the study of the relationships between, living things—should be viewed as the noblest science. Writing in 1857, Agassiz declared that the systems by which scientists classify plants and animals are "in truth but translations, into human language, of the thoughts of the Creator." And what did Agassiz infer about the creator from the myriads of organisms scattered over the Earth? Evidence of "premeditation, power, wisdom, greatness, prescience, omniscience, providence."

Just as technology has extended our vision to the stars, with both land-based and orbiting telescopes that can see to the dawn of time, so has it allowed us to see the world of cells and molecules that, through some alchemy that biologists are only beginning to fathom, can combine in just the right way to produce this mystery we call life. Individually, the microscopic ingredients of living things—bloblike blood vessels in the brainstem, the dancing worms that are the human chromosomes, the little rodeo arenas that are the energy-producing mitochondria of all cells—are fairly unassuming. Even the exquisite symmetries of the hormone oxytocin, whose secretion causes the uterus to contract during labor and also to stimulate the flow of milk in a nursing mother, give no hint of its talents. Most important, of course, none of the individual ingredients in a living being are themselves alive. Yet somehow—when the twisting strands of DNA and RNA interact with the beadlike strings of rudimentary proteins called polymers inside a semipermeable membrane—synergy is sparked, and they produce life.

That "somehow," of course, is the crux of a long-running debate. That lens proteins have just the right structure to refract light in the eye, that DNA has just the right structure to be self-replicating, strikes many people as approximately as likely to occur through chance and natural selection as (to borrow a favorite analogy of this school of thought) a junkyard full of airplane parts is to get whipped up by a passing gale and assemble themselves into a Boeing 767. This way of thinking is hugely appealing, even intuitive. The alternative—that complexity and variety arose through the Darwinian interplay of chance and selection working over billions of years—is dry, academic, counterintuitive. It is no surprise, then, that the Paley-like argument that biological complexity could not have arisen by chance, but must be the work of a divine creator, has many more adherents. This belief goes by the name "intelligent design," for the core tenet of this theory is that there exists an intelligence behind the wondrous designs we see in nature. If science were decided by popular vote, intelligent design would beat evolution in a landslide. Americans seem to overwhelmingly reject the Darwinian view of evolution: In Gallup polls taken throughout the 1990s, 45 percent of those responding (all adults) said they believed in the biblical view that God "created humans in their present form within the last 10,000 years." Even more of those answering, accepting evidence such as that from anthropology (with its four-million-year-old human fossils) and geophysics (which uses radioactive dating and other techniques to conclude that Earth is some five billion years old), agree that "humans have developed over millions of years from less-advanced forms of life, but God guided this process."

And those who believe that life arose and evolved through chemistry and physics in ways that do not require God to tinker with the process? All of 12 percent.

From its inception with Paley's *Natural Theology*, a favorite exemplum of intelligent design theorists has been the mammalian eye. Its appeal derives from its myriad of components, each of which is a paean to biological architecture in and of itself but all of which need to work in concert. What is most striking about the eye, argued Paley, is the perfect coordination of its components. Each is crucial for vision, yet none alone has much use. "Is it possible to believe," he wrote, "that the eye was formed without any regard to vision; that it was the animal itself which found out, that, though formed with no such intention, it would serve to see with; and that the use of the eye, as an organ of sight, resulted from this discovery, and the animals' application of it?" To Paley and his philosophical descendants, the answer was and is a clear "no": it is not possible to believe such a thing.

Now the sense of wonder inspired by the beauty and complexity of the eye and the rest of the natural world has been harnessed in the service of the 21st-century version of intelligent design. It is impossible to imagine, goes this way of thinking, how the iris, the lens, the cornea, the retina, the optic nerve, and all the rest of the organ of sight could have evolved separately into the complex components that they are today since, without each of the other components, no single component would have served any

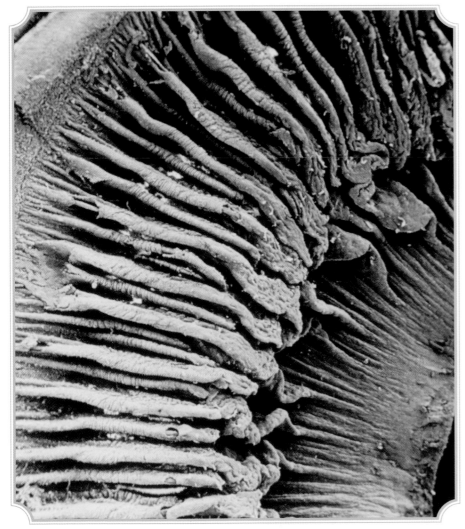

The Ciliary Body & Iris—*The deeply folded tissue at left and top is the ciliary body, which normally encircles and controls the lens of the eye, flattening it to focus distant objects onto the retina and making it more spherical to focus closer ones. In this view, seen from the back of the eye, the lens has been removed. As a result, one can see through to the less folded muscles of the iris, which controls the aperture of the pupil (the black area at bottom right) and the amount of light that reaches the retina.*

purpose. A cornea without a retina doesn't confer much survival advantage, say proponents of intelligent design, so Darwinian evolution would have had nothing on which to exert selective pressure. Yet somehow each of these parts arose and was assembled into a functioning eye, much like a car maker brings together a working engine from over here, a working fuel pump from there, a functional air bag system—each a fully operational component to be assembled into the automobile. In this sense, the components of the eye are "irreducibly" complex. The conclusion: just as an intelligent designer draws up plans for the components of an automobile and sees that those plans are executed, so must an intelligent designer have ordered up the components of the eye.

Fifty-seven years after Paley's book, Charles Darwin's *The Origin of Species* offered a mechanism by which simplicity could give rise to complexity. Nevertheless, Paley's arguments have had tremendous staying power. As the millennium turned, in fact, opponents of teaching evolution in the public schools backed away from their insistence that creationism be taught alongside evolution—an argument that the courts, citing the First Amendment's prohibition against the government establishment of religion, keep rejecting. Instead, they pushed for teaching intelligent design theory.

The current reincarnation of intelligent design has been spearheaded by biochemist Michael J. Behe, whose 1996 book, *Darwin's Black Box,* lays out the argument for design. He focuses on the organelles within a cell and the biochemistry they support. The organelles are nothing less than intricate little machines, he notes, constructed from proteins that the cell itself synthesizes. These living machines carry on the functions that, when combined with those of other little machines in other cells of a body, add up to life. Behe's fundamental premise is that the organelles and proteins—his human examples are blood-clotting, the immune system, and the system within cells to transport proteins and other molecules around and beyond the cell—exhibit the same "irreducible complexity" as the eye. The "complexity" part is noncontroversial, as the photographs in the following pages attest to so beautifully. It's the "irreducible" part that stirs debate. By "irreducible," Behe and other partisans of intelligent design mean that no single component of the eye brings any benefit without the presence of all the others; how, then, could any of them have been selected for? Similarly, how could such cellular machinery have evolved in piecemeal fashion through a series of adaptations, as Darwinism holds?

One of Behe's favorite examples is the flagellum of sperm and some bacteria. This whiplike appendage serves as a propeller of sorts, scooting the sperm or bacterium through whatever liquid medium it finds itself in. Yet for the flagellum to work, argues Behe, it needs all of its component parts. How, then, can natural selection bring about a flagellum? Natural selection works in the present, not the future, he points out: it can give "thumbs up" or "thumbs down" to various chance changes as they come along, depending on whether those incremental changes add to or subtract from the fitness of the organism. That is, each part as it arises gets the gladiator-in-the-Coliseum treatment: it lives or dies based on its own merits. Evolution does not wait around to discover which other components might happen along, to combine with existing ones to increase or decrease fitness. New components don't pass the test of natural selection based on the possibility that some other component might happen along in a few millennia and combine with the first to produce something useful.

That presents a conundrum: Of what possible use is part of a flagellum? None at all, Behe contends: a partially formed flagellum is approximately as useful, propulsion-wise, as a piston without a drive shaft. It therefore could not have been produced by the mechanism of natural selection acting upon random changes resulting from genetic mutation, the Darwinian paradigm. Instead, there must a designer. The flagellum and similar examples of irreducible complexity, he concludes, emit "a loud, clear, piercing cry of design"—and hence of the same designer, or "contriver," that Paley saw almost two centuries before.

But the premise of this "irreducible complexity" argument is "factually wrong," argues Kenneth R. Miller, a cell biologist. When, in 2002, the state of Ohio was considering requiring public schools to teach intelligent design, he testified before the legislature against the proposal. Although Miller quite definitely believes in "a reality that transcends the material," he says, he also believes that the mechanisms of mutation and natural selection can account for all the splendors of the living world.

What Behe and other intelligent designers regard as useless bits and pieces—the components of useful structures like the flagellum or the eye—are nothing of the sort, Miller says. Instead, even these unassuming components can have, even before they are components, other uses. It's sort of like having some wires, circuit boards, lasers, and other parts lying around: even before you assemble them into, say, a CD player, you might find perfectly good use for them in something simpler like a radio. In fact, some of the most interesting research on this has been done on that "irreducibly complex" organ, the eye. As you remember, Paley argued that because an organism has no use for a retina alone, or for an iris alone, or (at the molecular level of analysis where his intellectual descendants have advanced the argument from design) for the specially-functioning proteins that compose these structures, then their presence in a functioning assembly such as the eye testifies to design. Again, the reason is that none of the components alone confers any adaptive advantage, and so could not have been selected by evolution to hang around until other components of the eye, similarly selected by evolution, were in place to produce the entire assemblage.

But the premise of that argument is incorrect for at least one of the biomolecules that play a role in the eye: the crystallin proteins of the lens. The crystallins make up about 90 percent of the soluble proteins of the eye lenses of most vertebrates. They had long been considered "especially chosen and designed for their ability to confer the required refractive properties onto the transparent lens," as J. Piatigorsky told a society of ophthalmologists in 1993. "We have grown up with the idea that crystallins are as specialized as the eye itself." More recent studies, however, have shown that the crystallins originally had a quite different function. It turns out that the cell is an opportunist if ever there was one. It can co-opt proteins that originally evolved for one purpose and turn them to a different purpose. In the argot of evolutionary biology, this is called an "exaptation," a term coined by Stephen Jay Gould and Elisabeth Vrba in 1982. An exaptation is a trait that arose for one reason but is co-opted for a new one. It is useful (aptus) as a result of (ex) its form. Through exaptation, the cell can build up its complicated little machines from specialized components, and that seems to be what happened with crystallins. Although they now help form the structure of the lens and refract light, some of the crystallins are close cousins of so-called heat shock proteins, and others are near-copies of metabolic and other enzymes. They were already lying around, serving other purposes. To evolutionary biologists, this discovery makes it that much easier to imagine how natural processes could have gathered up such components and assembled them into something with as many complicated parts as the eye.

Gould had other pet examples of exaptations. One was the light organ of the squid, *Euprymna scolopes*. In it, the squid gathers phosphorescent bacteria that glow with light. The light organ also contains a lens, made of transparent tissue that refracts the light emitted by the glowing bacteria. Although it now serves this very specialized purpose, it turns out that this transparent tissue is merely a version of an enzyme that protects organisms against damage from deleterious biochemicals called peroxidases. It seems that this enzyme, although initially used for protection, was at some point converted in the squid and other species to serve a structural role in the lens of the eye.

"The whole notion of irreducible complexity doesn't stand up to scientific analysis," says Miller. "When you analyze the parts of these [structures], you find that most often the individual parts—or small assemblies of two or three of them—do indeed

have function. And because the individual parts have function, they can indeed be produced by Darwinian natural selection."

In 1999, for instance, biochemists discovered the remarkable "double life" of a human enzyme. Called tyrosyl-transfer RNA synthethase, this molecule catalyzes the reaction in which the amino acid tyrosine gets fished out of the cellular soup and attached to the transfer RNA molecule so that it can be added to a growing polypeptide chain like a pearl on a necklace. Surely, this is a highly specialized function, one that would have no adaptive advantage if the cell did not also have tyrosine, ribosomes, and all the other components of its protein-making machinery. According to the argument from design, then, the appearance of this enzyme independent of the rest of that machinery strains credulity. Yet, as the biochemists discovered, this enzyme is remarkably similar to another molecule that performs a very different function: attracting scavenger cells to cells that are committing suicide.

Needless to say, one can believe in a divine being without also believing that said being fiddles with life every step of the way. One can be both a person of faith and an adherent of evolution. During the Ohio debate, the *Columbus Dispatch* newspaper printed one missive it received on a postcard with no return address:

"Dear [State Legislator] Linda Reidelbach," it read. "Evolution is one of my creations with which I am most pleased. Signed, God."

To people who see the world this way, scientists as well as non-scientists, the intricacy of life's ingredients is itself a source of awe. One of these scientists is evolutionary biologist Francisco J. Ayala. A man of faith, Ayala criticizes intelligent design less for what it says about biology than for what it says about God. To contend that a supreme being designed the human eye and other complex biological organs, says Ayala, amounts to blasphemy. "If our organs were designed by somebody, that person was very clumsy, outright stupid, and much worse than any human engineer," he says. As evidence, he offers the human jaw. As orthodontists know all too well, the jaw is too small to accommodate all our teeth. That's because some two million years ago human ancestors began to grow larger brains, which required larger heads to contain them. That's fine once the person is out in the world, but for a woman to deliver a large-headed baby is a prescription for disaster: the birth canal is not large enough for a larger-all-around head to fit through. Women's pelvic regions changed in a way that would accommodate the larger-brained baby, but so did the baby's head: the human jaw became smaller, with the result that our teeth often don't fit. "What engineer would do such a lousy job?" asks Ayala. "I would not want to do anything with a God who would design things so badly."

Biologist Kenneth Miller, who is also an observant Roman Catholic, has similar concerns. If God intentionally designed 30 species of Equus that eventually became extinct, as well as 23 dress rehearsals for elephants over the last five million years (including wooly mammoths and mastodons, as the fossil record shows), then God's most obvious trait is incompetence. "He can't make it right the first time," says Miller. "I don't think the Almighty works that way." Such designs are "distinctly substandard, because nearly every one became extinct. If you want to accept intelligent design, you'd damn well better account for" the countless failed species down through the eons. More likely, says Miller, is a bumbling process like evolution, in which random mutations throw out all sorts of suggestions but natural selection allows only a favored few to survive—and even that, only until conditions change and the selective forces change.

Stephen Jay Gould, who died in the spring of 2002, makes a similar appeal. The argument from design implies a divine creator who is elegant and efficient. Yet so much of the natural world is anything but, Gould argued, asking what sort of creator would design so many imperfections into the biological world. Organisms are rife with maladaptive features. Our genome's three billion or so chemical units are mostly padding: less than one percent of those units do the work of coding for proteins, while the rest are so-called junk DNA. What's the purpose of that? The frigate bird has webbed feet, yet never paddles, making those feet a nice enough adornment but basically extraneous. Why have 99.99 percent of the species that have ever walked, flown, swum, slithered, or crawled on Earth gone extinct—surely God wasn't such a bad designer that virtually everything he put his hand to had to be thrown away. In a chapter he contributed to a book just before his death, Gould wrote, "Odd arrangements and funny solutions are the proof of evolution—paths that a sensible God would never tread but that a natural process, constrained by history, follows perforce."

To take the argument one step further: Among these imperfections and odd arrangements are we to include what we might call biological evil? Would the appearance of cancer cells, for example, be better accounted for by "a natural process" or by a divine designer?

Indeed, some theologians argue that the propensity of some cells to break through the controls on their replication and begin multiplying uncontrollably is an expression of the promise in the Bible. In Genesis, notes Carl Feit, a cancer biologist and Talmudic scholar at Yeshiva University in New York, God is described as creating the world in an incomplete and even imperfect state. He presents Adam and Eve with a challenge: to fill the world and achieve dominion over it. "This wondrous universe that He created was in an incomplete state," Feit says. "So He challenged man to be His partner in bringing the creation to completion and perfection. Imperfection includes disease. That's why traditional Judaism regards the conquest of disease as

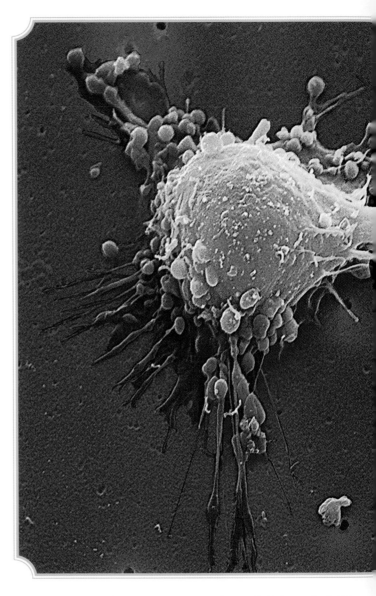

Cancer Cell Division—*These two prostate cancer cells are in the final stage of cell division (cytokinesis), during which the cells' cytoplasm divides. Here the cells are joined by a thin cytoplasmic bridge. Cancer cells divide rapidly in a chaotic, uncontrolled manner and may clump to form tumors, which invade and destroy surrounding tissues.*

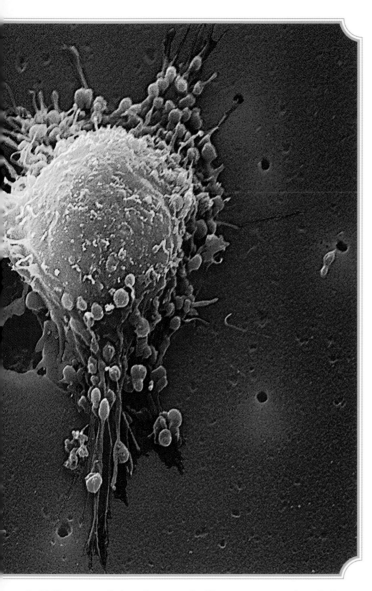

general one of evil, part of whose answer involves free will: that to choose goodness doesn't really count if choosing evil is precluded by divine fiat. So, too, with cancer. "God stepped back from his creation," Feit says, "and has given the universe a freedom in how it plays out. God knew what He was doing, so I have to assume this is the world He wanted to create."

As theologians wrestle with the existence of biological evil, scientists have their own take on it. Cancer arises when something goes awry during the process of cell division called mitosis. One bit of DNA gets excised, another bit substitutes for what was there originally, still another bit gets duplicated more than it should. There are, in fact, multiple ways for a cell to become malignant, but all derive from mistakes during replication. Yet mistakes are also the foundation on which evolutionary change—dare we say evolutionary progress?—is based. Evolution, you recall, builds on chance mutations in DNA. Most such changes are deleterious or even deadly, and the organism dies. But a rare few mutations produce a change that is beneficial to the organism and, if the change occurs in the DNA of a sperm or an egg, to all its descendants, too. These are the beneficial mutations that gave aquatic creatures lungs and enabled them to leave the water and colonize the land; these are the mutations that produced a lineage of naked apes from an ape ancestor shared by today's humans and other primates; these are the changes that are, in short, the raw material of evolution. "That imperfection

a fulfillment of the divine challenge." But why did God create this imperfection for humans to deal with in the first place? The question echoes the more

is the basis for the wondrous variety of life we have in the world today," says Feit. Cancer, the result of those same sorts of mutations, is the price we pay for having the raw material of evolution.

More generally, the argument from design leaves some theologians uneasy because it is a throwback to an earlier way of thinking called "the God of the gaps." This was an appeal to belief based on ignorance. That is, when natural phenomena defied man's attempts at understanding, he attributed them to God. This ploy has obvious drawbacks, however: the more humans figured out about their world, the smaller were the "gaps" (of knowledge) into which they could put their god. When the genesis of thunder and lightning was a mystery, people explained frightening storms as the manifestations of heavenly battles. When scientists could not explain the origins of the Earth, the galaxy, or the entire cosmos, they attributed their formation to God. But once meteorologists explained thunderstorms as the children of colliding air masses, and once geophysicists explained the origins of the Earth from a condensing cloud of gas and dust, and once astrophysicists explained the birth of galaxies from minuscule density fluctuations that appeared when the universe was a mere 300,000 years old (compared to the 13 billion or 14 billion years that it is today), and once cosmologists started building a theory of the beginning of the universe—well, even if all of these mysteries and all of these origins are not completely understood, the scientific understanding seemed to be leaving decidedly less room for a deity. Yet that is where intelligent design starts. Its examples are more complex than "where does lightning come from?" but the fundamental premise is the same: "Science has not explained how this happened, and I surely don't understand how it came about, so God must have done it." Or as British biologist Richard Dawkins puts it, "the argument from personal incredulity"— which says that if you can't imagine how some phenomenon (like biological complexity) came about naturally then it couldn't have happened—is a pretty weak foundation for faith.

To some, the appeal to science is so much sound and fury signifying nothing: Why spin ludicrous theories about big bangs and quantum fluctuations when, as any sensible person knew, the answer to the puzzle of the creation of the world was right there in Genesis. To that, philosopher Michael Ruse offers an answer. By refusing to cry miracle in the face of natural mysteries, modern science has brought the world "fantastic dividends." To attribute divine causes when naturalistic ones might be just over the next scientific horizon is dubious theology. For one thing, surely faith should rest on something more profound than ignorance. For another, intelligent design assumes restrictions on God's creativity. "To try to suggest that God couldn't do things through natural selection or through evolution seems to me to be horrendously limiting" to his power, Ruse says.

Intelligent design "fails as much, if not more, on theological grounds as on scientific grounds."

As proponents of intelligent design amass examples of "irreducible complexity," and proponents of evolution by chance mutation and natural selection find counterexamples like lens crystallin proteins that got co-opted from an earlier function in order to serve a new, more complex one, a handful of psychologists, psychiatrists and neuroscientists are pursuing a wholly different approach to the search for the mind of God: they are looking for evidence of it in the human brain. Consider one experiment run at the University of Pennsylvania. In a small, unlit enclosure just off the main part of the lab, a young man who is accomplished in the techniques of Tibetan Buddhist meditation touches a match to a stick of jasmine incense and to several candles. He makes himself comfortable on the floor, settling into the lotus position. He begins to meditate. As is his practice, he starts by quieting the chatter in his consciousness and trying to lose himself in an inner, spiritual reality far from the material world. He holds a length of cotton twine in his fingertips. At the other end of the twine, which runs beneath the closed door and into the adjacent room, sit two scientists. Dr. Andrew Newberg, who specializes in brain scans, has wrapped the end loosely around his finger. Beside him sits Dr. Eugene d'Aquili, a longtime assistant professor in the Department of Psychiatry, who had spent years researching the correlation between religious states and brain function. They are waiting for the young man to tug on his end of the twine. That's the signal that he has reached the peak of spiritual intensity.

As usual during his meditation sessions, the young man's mind becomes quiet, allowing what he describes as a deeper and less encumbered part of himself to emerge. When it does, the young man says, he suddenly sees that "his inner self is not an isolated entity, but that he is inextricably connected to all of creation," as Newberg puts it in the 2001 book he co-authored, *Why God Won't Go Away*. "There's a sense of timelessness and infinity," the young man told the scientists. "It feels like I am part of everyone and everything in existence."

After an hour, Newberg feels the tug. On cue, he injects a radioactive tracer into a long intravenous line that parallels the cotton twine, snaking out of the lab, into the meditation room and into a vein in the young man's left arm. Within a few moments, the young man has ended his meditation, and the two scientists run into the room and whisk him off to a hulking SPECT (single photon emission computer tomography) camera, which detects the radioactive tracer that blood flow has carried into the young man's brain and which gloms onto neurons in the brain. Because heightened neuronal activity is correlated with increased brain flow, concentrations of the radioactive tracer mark areas of the brain that are particularly active. The tracer sticks in place for hours, so whichever region was most active when the tracer reached the brain—in this case, just at the point of the young man's peak meditative state—will be caught and imaged by the SPECT camera. It produces a fascinating color image. Even a casual observer can see that an area of unusually high activity is concentrated at the top, rear of the left side of the brain. Neuroanatomists know it as the posterior ("back") superior ("top") parietal lobe (for the brain lobe it resides in). Newberg and d'Aquili have a more colloquial name for it: the orientation association area.

There are actually a pair of orientation areas, one in the brain's right hemisphere and one in the left. Previous studies have produced a fairly clear job description for these bundles of neurons, with some of the clearest evidence coming from people with lesions or other injury there. If your right orientation area is damaged, you struggle to determine angles and distances, and even which direction is up or down. You have trouble navigating in physical space: you can barely walk from bedroom door to bed, because as distances and angles and depths change continuously with every step, the brain is hopelessly confused. If your left orientation area suffers an injury, on the other hand, you cannot keep track of where your body is relative to the space beyond. As a result, you cannot gauge how to lower yourself into the bed: you have no sense of where you leave off and objects in the environment begin. You don't how far or fast to descend. The left orientation area, it

seems, creates the brain's sense of the physical extent of the body. Interestingly, some neurons in the left orientation area respond only to objects that the arm can reach; others are specialized for receiving sensory information only from more distant objects. This discovery has led to the hypothesis that the brain draws the boundary between the self and the outside world based on the left orientation area's talent for discriminating between these two categories of things. When the orientation area is intact, it receives constant input from the sense of sight and the sense of touch, which it uses to determine where the individual ends and the rest of the world begins. It is able to "keep tabs on the you—not your dichotomy," says Newberg.

Before the young man began to meditate, his orientation area was a hub of activity, as expected. But when he tugged on the twine, at the peak of his meditative state, his orientation area showed a strikingly different pattern of activity. According to the SPECT camera, when the young man felt "part of everyone and everything in existence," his orientation was as quiet as a churchmouse. One possibility, Newberg realized, was that the usual sensory information was not reaching the orientation area. Although it remained perfectly functional, at least in theory, if it were deprived of the sensory information from which it usually draws a picture of the outside world and determines where the individual ends and the outside world begins, then it would be like a cartographer without survey data: unable to produce an accurate map. And as meditators know, one of the goals of meditation is to quiet the flow of information from the senses by shutting your eyes, stilling outside noise, and concentrating inwardly rather than outwardly. "With no information flowing in from the sense," explains Newberg, the orientation area "wouldn't be able to find any boundaries. What would the brain make of that?" Perhaps the "failure to find the borderline between the self and the outside world" would be taken to mean "that such a distinction doesn't exist." The brain would "perceive that the self is endless and intimately interwoven with everyone and everything" in existence. And one more thing: this perception would feel completely, and indisputably, real.

Drs. Newberg and d'Aquili conducted the meditation experiment with seven other people who practiced Tibetan meditation. With only slight exceptions, the SPECT scans showed a quieting of activity in their orientation area when each reached a self-described peak moment of transcendence. The scientists later broadened the experiment to include a group of nuns belonging to the contemplative Franciscan order. As they did with the Tibetan meditators, the researchers had the nuns indicate when prayer had transported them to an intensely religious moment, at which point each woman was infused with the radioactive tracer and taken to the SPECT machine so her brain could be scanned for activity.

The nuns described this peak moment differently than the Buddhists did, characterizing it as "a tangible sense of the closeness of God and a mingling with him," Newberg says. What they experienced, interestingly enough, was an echo of what the 13th-century Franciscan nun Angela of Foligno described: "I . . . was led to a place in which I was united with God and was content with everything." The nuns' brains showed a pattern of activity virtually identical to that of the Buddhist meditators: their orientation area had gone quiet. Confronted with the absence of incoming sensory information, this specialized region of the brain apparently made do with what it had, constructing a reality in which the nuns felt like boundaries had melted away and that they had become one with God. The only difference between what the nuns experienced and what the Tibetan Buddhist meditators did was what lay beyond their sense of the physical boundaries of their own being: for the Buddhists, it was a sense of the universe; for the Franciscan nuns, it was an eternal, omnipotent, and loving deity.

Mystical experience, then, has a neurobiological basis. To some, that makes it somehow "more real," harder to dismiss as an illusion or a delusion, as wishful thinking, or plain old error. (Of course, each of those things is also a mental state with a biological basis, but one less specific than the muting of the orientation area.) This has led to two obvious possibilities.

One is that the wiring of the human brain leads to the illusion of transcendence and the presence of God, as skeptics argue. In this case, a bundle of neurons that ordinarily construct a sense of physical space and of the boundaries between self and non-self gets fooled by the cutoff of sensory information that people deep in prayer or meditation are unquestionably able to achieve. According to this argument, the response of those neurons is the sense of a melting away of the physical self until it is connected to all of the universe, or to God. But that connection has no basis in reality; it is an illusion born of sensory deprivation, of the brain struggling to make sense of the altered sensory input.

The other possibility is that the orientation area is what the mind of God bestowed on the brain of man so that puny humans could occasionally grasp the awesome existence of a deity, or, in other traditions, of a greater reality beyond the here and now. As with so many other places where science and religion intersect, there is no experimental or even logical way to distinguish between these two possibilities. To people of faith, that the mind of man is able to grasp the infinitude of God is further testimony to the care that the Creator took in assembling humankind. To agnostics, that the brain makes the leap from a temporary inability to tell where the self ends and the rest of the world begins inspires a sort of "aha" moment: so that's where the illusion of God comes from.

The human brain has at least one other built-in feature that reinforces belief: It is wired so that many aspects of religious ritual drive the mind to places it would otherwise never experience. It turns out that repetitive rhythms, be they the chants of a Latin mass or the call and response of a Baptist service or the continuously intoned mantra of a Buddhist meditator, affect both the limbic system and the autonomic nervous system. The limbic system is the group of brain structures, particularly the amygdala and the hypothalamus, that serve as the seat of emotion, taking in signals from the senses or from other regions of the brain and tagging them with an emotion like fear or joy or despair. The autonomic system's primary function is to run unconscious processes such as heart beat, blood pressure, and body temperature. Slow, quiet rituals such as incantatory group prayer can quiet the autonomic system, as witnessed by the slowing heart rate of many people deep in such prayer. The associated mental state is one of bliss and tranquility, often associated with a sense of proximity to a divine being.

Alternatively, hyperstimulating rituals such as the manic dancing of Sufi mystics can lead to an aroused mental state, one often described as channeling the wisdom of the cosmos. When the brain is excited in this way, a little horse-shaped structure called the hippocampus puts on the brakes, inhibiting neuronal transmission within the brain so that certain regions are deprived of their usual input.

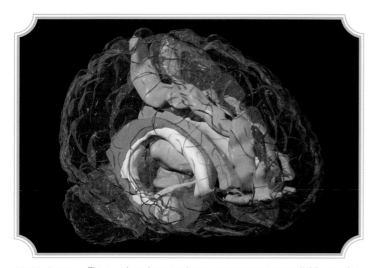

Limbic System—*This is a three-dimensional magnetic resonance imaging (MRI) scan of the limbic system of a healthy human brain. The front of the brain is at right. The limbic system is involved in instinct, emotion, and establishing memories. It consists of an arc of structures, such as the amygdala (light blue, lower center), that lie below the corpus callosum (green layer, center). The thalamus (purple), caudate nucleus (bright pink, part of the basal ganglia) and cingulate gyrus (pale pink, above the corpus callosum) are also seen.*

One of those structures is the orientation area, the one that goes quiet when Buddhist meditators and Franciscan nuns reach their peak of transcendence. Ritual, apparently, has a comparable power. Working through the autonomic system, it can drive the brain to such a state of arousal that the hippocampus shuts the gate, as it were, halting the flow of sensory data to the orientation area with the same result that the SPECT-scanned subjects in Newberg and d'Aquili's experiments described: a sense of the merging of the self with a greater power. Ritual can also induce a quieting of the orientation area directly, with the same result on the brain's ability to determine the boundaries of the self. Hence the

power of ritual, analogous to the power of individual prayer or meditation, to bring participants a sense of unity with those around them as well as something beyond them.

Although the exact mechanism by which rituals are able to induce either of these mental states—one hyperaroused and the other hyperquiescent—remains a mystery, the fact that they can induce a sense of transcendence and of a closing of the distance between the participant and God goes far toward explaining their power and their persistence through the millennia.

To see an expression of the mind of God in the forms and functions of living things, including the human brain, dates back at least two centuries, to William Paley and James McCosh and their refinements of natural theology. And although the details have changed, the general outlines of the refutation have remained much as they were in 1802. Just as Darwin himself did, his intellectual heirs argue that "design" in nature is relatively rare, which is one reason it stands out, and that imperfection and caprice predominate. And they argue, second, that instances of exquisite fit of form to function arise not from the benevolence of a Creator but as a side effect of mere evolution. Ursula Goodenough is a cell biologist, a distinguished scientist who is also a person of faith. In *The Sacred Depths of Nature*, she wrote that "the continuation of life reaches around, grabs its own tail, and forms a sacred circle that requires no further justification, no Creator, no superordinate meaning of meaning, no purpose other than that the continuation continue until the sun collapses or the final meteor collides. I confess a credo of continuation."

In the pages that follow, we hope to show you some of those "sacred depths." You will see the DNA of a cell's mitochondrion, extending its tendrils like a road pushing into the deepest green jungle. You will see crystalline forms of organic molecules, the rough-faceted topaz of human progesterone and the aqua tendrils of adenine, one of the four chemical bases that, in DNA, spell out the human genome. You will see photomicrographs of the protein actin, looking for all the world like the luminescent wing of a butterfly backlit by the moon, as well as of human embryos at many points in gestation: the raspberry-like ball of cells of the human blastocyst, subject of so much controversy because it is the source of stem cells, and the eight-week-old embryo floating in the amniotic sac. Some of these pictures of life give no hint of the power of the subject they capture: the synapse—the point where two neurons in the human brain meet and communicate, forming the basis for moving, thinking, feeling, seeing, hearing, smelling, and tasting—presents a decidedly modest appearance. So do neurons: their transmission lines, or axons, look hardly more impressive than the trunk lines of an old phone system. Yet neurons and the synapses where they meet are the basis for the electrical and chemical signals within the brain that the mind transforms into memories and dreams, joy and despair, and the cognition that distinguishes humans from other animals.

Many of the historical attacks on science by traditional religion, in Galileo's day no less than in our own, rest on the assumption that science and faith are mutually exclusive. But a strong undercurrent of faith—if by faith we include a sense of the spiritual as well as simple awe in the creation—indeed runs through science. You can feel it in the way biologists talk about the extraordinary fit between structure and function in DNA, the molecule of heredity, and in their discovery of the fantastic choreography of chemistry that supports the reactions of the living cell. Creationists often charge evolutionary biologists with "worshiping at the church of Darwin." They intend that as an insult. But it is just as possible to see the sacred in the science of life as to find it in more traditional places, as Ursula Goodenough's words attest. Life is indeed a place of sacred depths; the microphotographs that follow bring them to the surface for everyone to appreciate.

Neurons (nerve cells) in the Human Cerebral Cortex—*Neurons exist in varying sizes and shapes throughout the nervous system. A basic neuron consists of a cell body with processes of two types: a single axon (the output, effector nerve fiber) and one or more dendrites, smaller, input processes that serve as sensory receptors. In the cerebral cortex, neurons of comparable structure are arranged in a variable number of distinct layers.*

If faith has meaning it can't be off in one part of you. It has to be integrated. I think my faith adds to the experience of being a scientist in the way that discovering something has more meaning, sort of glimpsing the mind of God.

FRANCIS COLLINS
Geneticist

DNA—A sample of uncoated, double-stranded DNA was dissolved in a salt solution and deposited on graphite to create this image. The row of orange and yellow peaks represents the ridges of the double helix in the short section of this right-handed DNA molecule.

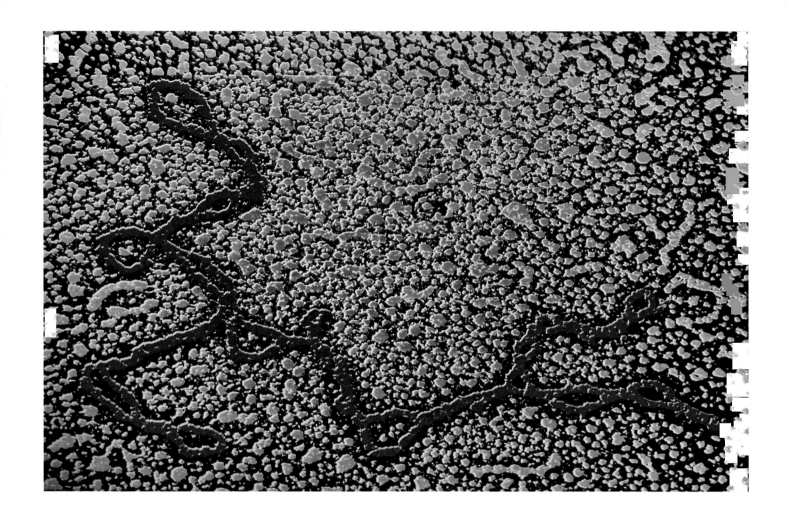

Whatever name you give to the origin of man, this spiritual quality of humans to understand, feel, and exist, it is holy, it is divine, and therefore, it should be eternal.

 CICERO

DNA from a Mitochondrion—*This is the site of synthesis of chemical energy within the cell. The filament seen in this image was collected from a fragmented mitochondrion. This relatively tiny amount of DNA is estimated to have a coding capacity of about 5,000 amino acids, and suggests that the mitochondrion needs to rely on a supplement of external DNA (from the cell nucleus) to synthesize its constituents.*

We may explore the universe and find ourselves, or we may explore ourselves and find the universe. It matters not which of these paths we choose.

◸ DIANA ROBERTSON

The only real voyage of discovery consists not in seeking new landscapes, but in having new eyes.

◸ UNKNOWN

Crystals of Progesterone—*This female sex hormone is secreted monthly in the ovary and stimulates development of the uterus to receive a fertilized egg and to nourish the embryo. In pregnancy, progesterone prevents menstruation and the release of more eggs; this characteristic of progesterone is the basis of the contraceptive pill.*

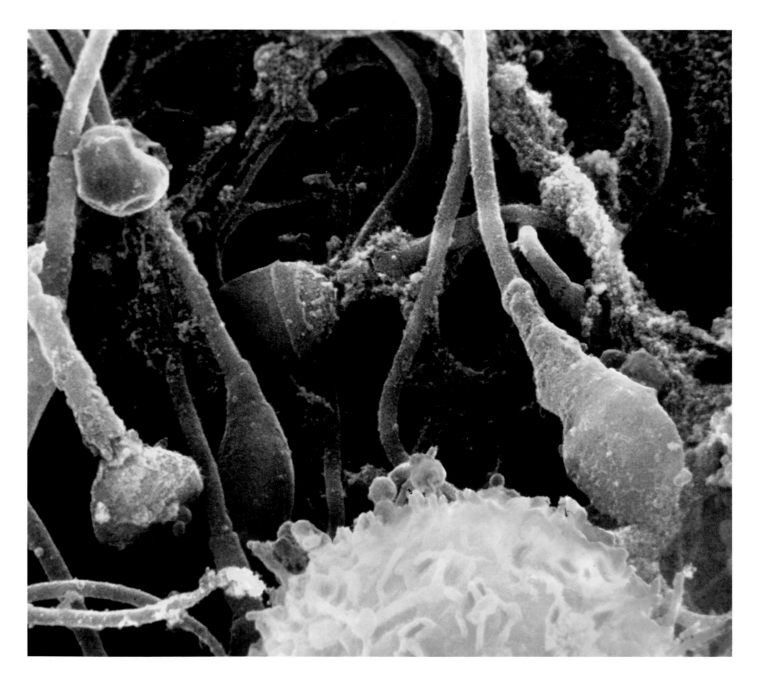

When a faithful thinker, resolute to detach every object from personal relations and see it in the light of thought, shall, at the same time, kindle science with the fire of the holiest affections, then will God go forth anew into the creation.

❧ RALPH WALDO EMERSON
Nature

It may be that there is no God, that "the existence of all that is beautiful and in any sense good is but the accidental and ineffective byproduct of blindly swirling atoms," that we are alone in a world that cares nothing for us or for the values that we create and sustain—that we and they are here for a moment only, and gone, and that eventually there will be left no trace of us in the universe. A man may well believe that this dreadful thing is true. But only the fool will say in his heart that he is glad that it is true.

❧ STERLING M. MCMURRIN
Professor of history and philosophy

Sperm over Early Embryo—*Sperm clustered over part of a 4-cell human embryo. Even though the egg has been fertilized, sperm (yellow) are still attached to the surface of the developing embryo. Each sperm has a head and a long tail. They are attached to the zone pellucida (green), the membrane which contains the embryo. Colored blue (at bottom) is a cumulus oophorus cell. Cumulus cells entirely surround the egg, providing the correct microenvironment for fertilization. Sperm must penetrate the cumulus cell layer to fertilize the egg.*

There are a limitless number of different sciences, but without one basic science, that is, what is the meaning of life and what is good for the people, all other forms of knowledge and art become idle and harmful entertainment.

LEO TOLSTOY
A Calendar of Wisdom

Methionine *is an important amino acid that helps to initiate the translation of messenger RNA. This sulfur-containing amino acid is also the source of sulfur for cysteine in animals and man. In that regard, methionine is considered an essential amino acid whereas cysteine is not; so cysteine is nonessential only as long as the diet contains adequate amounts of methionine.*

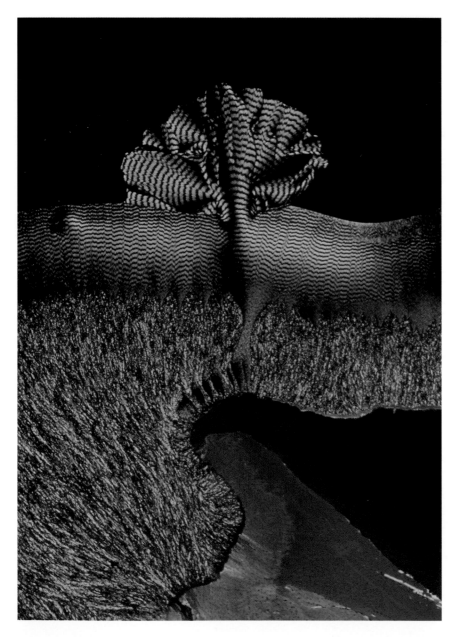

The masters of life know the Way, for they listen to the voice within them, the voice of wisdom and simplicity, the voice that reasons beyond Cleverness and knows beyond Knowledge.

THE TAO OF POOH

Male Sex Hormone—*Testosterone is the main human androgen responsible for the development of male reproductive organs and secondary sex characteristics. It is mainly produced in the testes by the action of a series of enzymes on pregnenolone, a steroid derived from cholesterol. Testosterone may be used in hormone replacement therapy to treat delayed puberty in boys, hypogonadism, and some types of impotence. In women, testosterone may be effective in the treatment of breast cancer.*

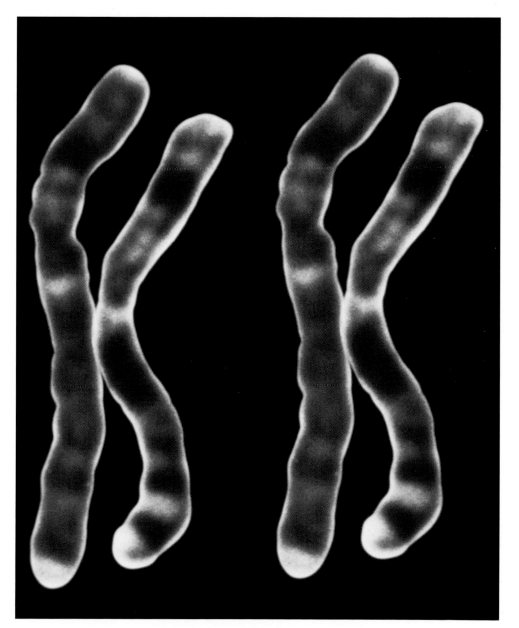

He has made everything beautiful in its time; also he has put eternity into man's mind, yet so that he cannot find out what God has done from the beginning to the end.

⌐   ECCLESIASTES 3:11

Female Sex Chromosomes—*Colored light micrograph of the two X chromosomes of a human female. Every human cell has 46 chromosomes, of which 22 pairs are identical in both males and females. However, in females the last pair comprises two X chromosomes, while males have one X and a much smaller Y chromosome. Chromosomes carry genetic information in the form of genes and the sex chromosomes carry the genes which control sexual development.*

Science does not have appropriate tools for the dissection of the spirit. How sad it would be, I thought, if we humans ultimately were to lose all sense of mystery, all sense of awe, if our left brains were utterly to dominate the right so that logic and reason triumphed over intuition and alienated us absolutely from our innermost being, from our hearts, from our souls.

JANE GOODALL
A Reason for Hope: A Spiritual Journey

Human Embryo on the Tip of a Pin—*This human embryo at the 10-cell stage, about three days old, is in the early stage of transformation from a single cell to a human composed of millions of cells. The ball of cells (orange) of the embryo is known as a morula, a cluster of almost identical, rounded cells, each containing a central nucleus. The cells multiply by repeated cleavage divisions (mitosis) and will form a hollow ball of cells (the blastocyst). Development of the blastocyst occurs before the embryo implants into the wall of the uterus (womb).*

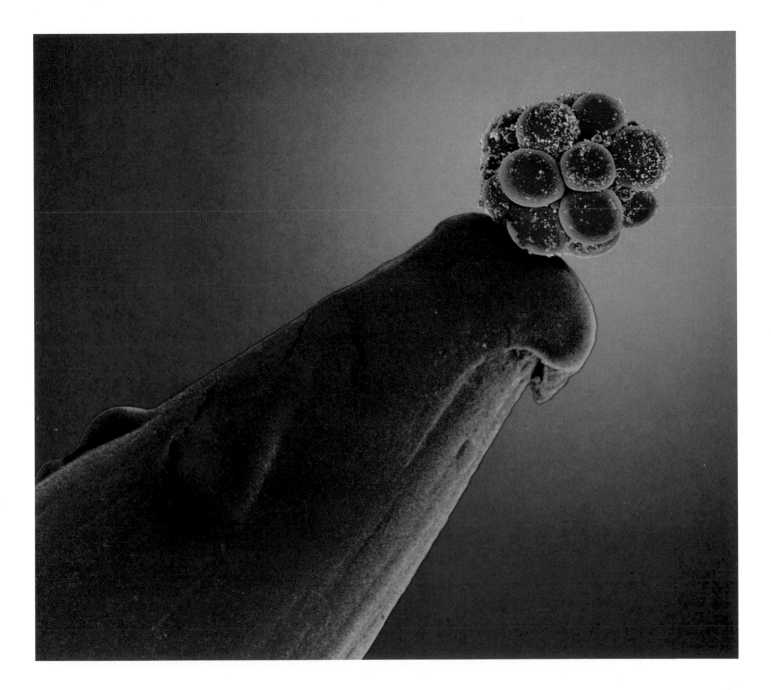

God gave us a curiosity to understand his creation. I don't think we need to worry that we will move into an exploration that will embarrass him.

⌐ FRANCIS COLLINS
Geneticist

DNA Single Crystal—*Grown from aqueous saline solution, this DNA single crystal demonstrates birefringence and the beginning of a focal conic texture. The DNA concentration for this specimen is unknown but is presumed to be in the neighborhood of 400 milligrams per millimeter.*

Female Sex Hormone—*This micrograph of 17-alpha-hydroxyprogesterone, also known as 17aOHP, one of the naturally occurring progestagens, is associated with the preparation of the body for pregnancy. 17aOHP is secreted in the ovaries, where it is synthesized by the action of enzymes on pregnenolone. It may be further processed by the body to produce androgens, estrogens, or corticosteroids. A synthetic form may be used to prevent miscarriage and to treat menstrual disorders.*

God does not require you to follow His leadings on blind trust. Behold the evidence of an invisible intelligence pervading everything, even your own mind and body.

❧   RAYMOND HOLLIWELL   ☙

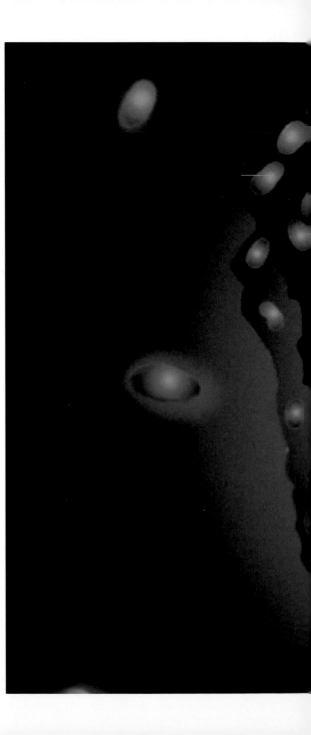

Educators may bring upon themselves unnecessary travail by taking a tactless and unjustifiable position about the difference between scientific and religious narratives. We see this, of course, in the conflict concerning creation science. Some representing, as they think, the conscience of science act much like those legislators who in 1925 prohibited by law the teaching of evolution in Tennessee. In that case, anti-evolutionists were fearful that a scientific idea would undermine religious belief. Today, pro-evolutionists are fearful that a religious idea will undermine scientific belief. The former had insufficient confidence in religion; the latter insufficient confidence in science. The point is that profound but contradictory ideas may exist side by side, if they are constructed from different materials and methods and have different purposes. Each tells us something important about where we stand in the universe, and it is foolish to insist that they must despise each other.

NEIL POSTMAN
The End of Education

Illustration of Embryo—*This illustration shows an example of the embryo at the two-cell stage. Cell division (mitosis) begins as the egg divides (cleaves) to form two cells. This first division, or cleavage, marks the initiation of development, and the zygote is now known as an embryo. The two cells produced by the cleavage are known as blastomeres.*

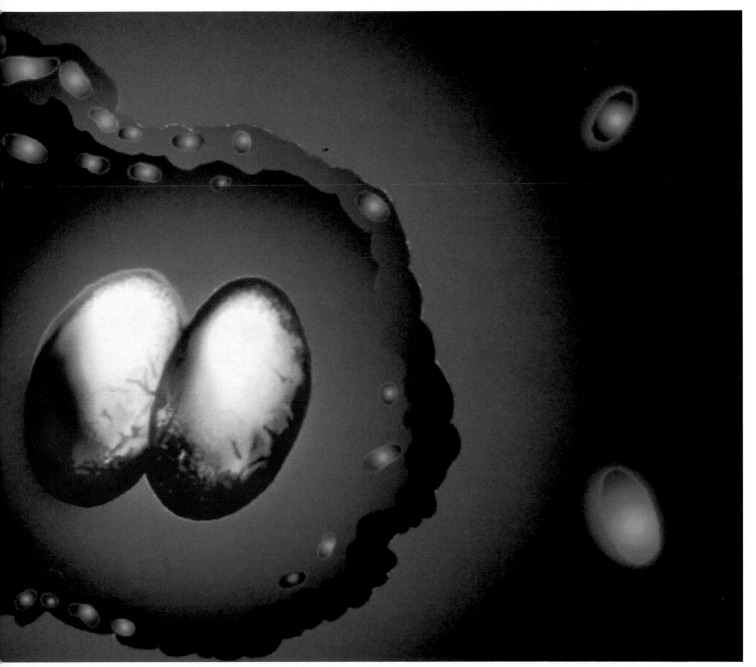

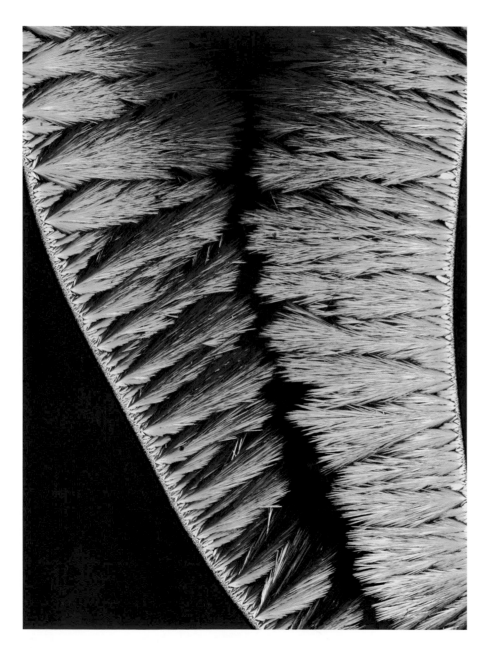

The miracles of the church seem to me to rest not so much upon faces or voices or healing power coming suddenly near to us from afar off, but upon our perceptions being made finer, so that for a moment our eyes can see and our ears can hear what is there about us always.

WILLA CATHER

Death Comes for the Archbishop

Crystals of Adenine (6-aminopurine)—*Adenine is an important member of the purine family of nucleic acid bases. It is one of the four bases found, as nucleotides, in the structure of DNA and RNA, materials which carry "genetic coding" in cells.*

L ife becomes religious whenever we make it so: when some new light is seen, when some deeper appreciation is felt, when some larger outlook is gained, when some nobler purpose is formed, when some task is well done.

❡ SOPHIA LYON FAHS
   Geneticist

Crystalline Cytosine (C) is one of the four organic bases of DNA. Pairs of bases, connected by hydrogen bonds, join the two strands of nucleotides which comprise the DNA double-helix molecule. It is a precise sequence of bases along a section of DNA that represents the genetic coding for a specific protein. Sections of DNA with such identifiable attributes are called genes.

Being religious means asking passionately the question of the meaning of our existence and being willing to receive answers, even if the answers hurt.

PAUL TILLICH
Saturday Evening Post

Wisdom begins in wonder.

⚔   SOCRATES   ⚔

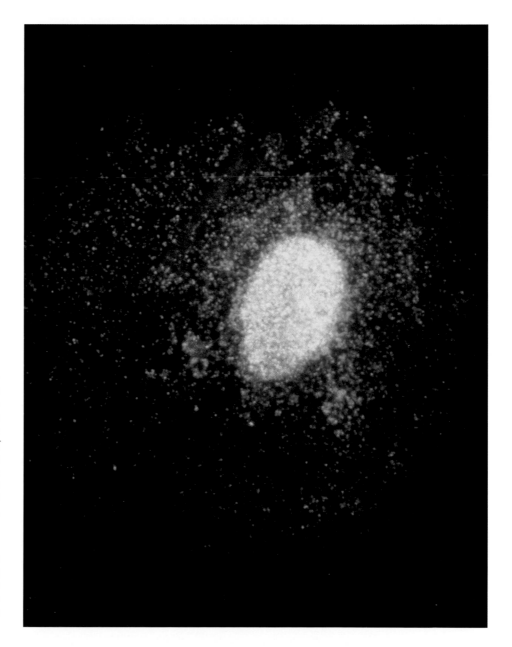

Mitosis—*In this image of a dividing cell nucleus, the chromosomes, containing all the genetic information of the organism, are stained red. During the process of cell division (mitosis) the chromosomes duplicate themselves to form two identical sets. As the cell divides, the chromosomes align themselves in the center of the nucleus, and one-half of each pair is pulled to opposite sides by a network of very thin fibers called the mitotic spindle (stained yellow/green). In this picture, all of the chromosome pairs have divided except for one which is still in the process of being pulled apart. Once this is complete the cell will cleave into two, separating the sets of chromosomes.*

DNA Migration—*In this fluorescent image, the cell nucleus is seen as a yellow mass at upper center, and migrating fragments of DNA are seen around the cell as yellow-green granules. This fluorescence of DNA has been caused by a process known as in-situ hybridization, which allows the location of DNA molecules within a normal cell to be assessed.*

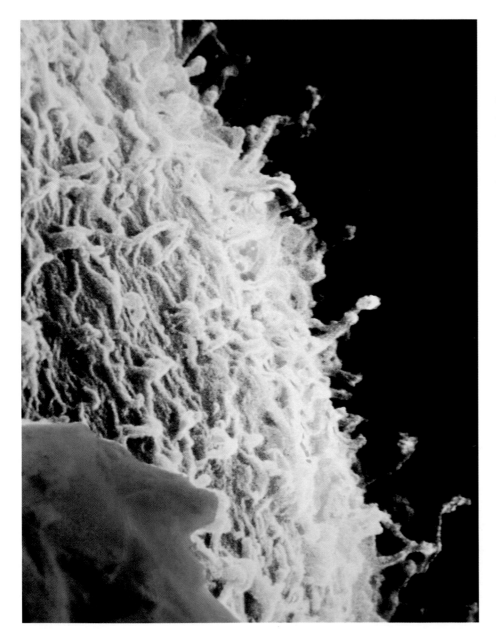

Science has a simple faith, which transcends utility. Nearly all men of science, all men of learning for that matter, and men of simple ways too, have it in some form and in some degree. It is the faith that it is the privilege of man to learn to understand, and that this is his mission. If we abandon that mission under stress we shall abandon it forever, for stress will not cease. Knowledge for the sake of understanding, not merely to prevail, that is the essence of our being. None can define its limits, or set its ultimate boundaries.

VANNEVAR BUSH
The Search for Understanding:
Science Is Not Enough

Embryo Surface—*This embryo is at the 2-4 cell stage, the egg having completed only one or two divisions after fertilization. The surface of the individual cell in the embryo are called blastomeres, and is covered with numerous tiny projections called microvilli, which greatly increase the surface area of the cell and indicate the high metabolic activity of the cell.*

Actin Stress Fibers—*Actin stress fibers, shown in red, are protein structures that help to give this cultured fibroblast cell its characteristic shape. Fibroblasts are cells that help to form connective tissues such as skin, tendons, cartilage, and ligaments.*

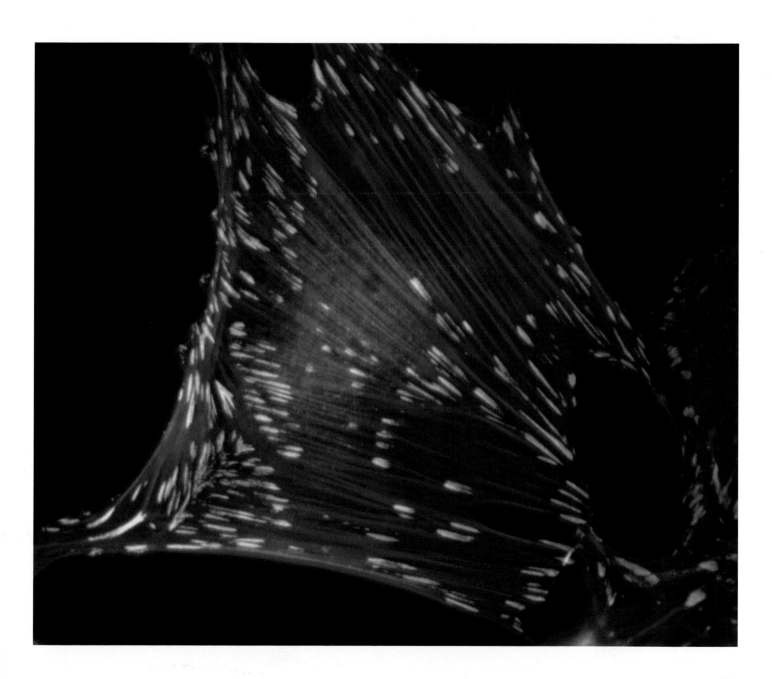

What is it that confers the noblest delight? What is that which swells a man's breast with pride above that which any other experience can bring to him? Discovery! To know that you are walking where none others have walked; that you are beholding what human eye has not seen before; that you are breathing a virgin atmosphere. To give birth to an idea—an intellectual nugget, right under the dust of a field that many a brain-plow had gone over before. To be the first—that is the idea. To do something, say something, see something, before anybody else—these are the things that confer a pleasure compared with other pleasures are tame and commonplace, other ecstasies cheap and trivial. Lifetimes of ecstasy crowded into a single moment.

MARK TWAIN
The Innocents Abroad

Oxytocin—*In women this hormone, secreted naturally by the pituitary gland, causes contractions of the uterus during labor, and it also stimulates the flow of milk in women who are breast-feeding. Produced synthetically, it may be used to induce childbirth or to help expel the placenta. Oxytocin may be given in the form of a nasal spray to help increase milk flow while breast-feeding.*

To suppose that the eye with all its inimitable contrivances for adjusting the focus to different distances, for admitting different amounts of light, and for the correction of spherical and chromatic aberration, could have been formed by natural selection, seems, I confess, absurd in the highest degree.

CHARLES DARWIN
The Origin of Species

One thing I have no worry about is whether God exists. But it has occurred to me that God has Alzheimer's and has forgotten we exist.

JANE WAGNER
The Search for Intelligent Life in the Universe,
performed by Lily Tomlin

Iris of the Eye—*This shows the inner surfaces of the iris and adjoining structures in the human eye. At far right (blue) is the edge of the pupil, the hole that allows light into the eye. Colored mauve is the iris which controls the size of the pupil and therefore how much light will enter. The bands of folds down the center (red) are the ciliary processes. These secrete fluids that nourish neighboring parts of the eye. They are also the sites of attachment for the long, thin zonule filaments (yellow and green) which are responsible for suspending the lens (unseen).*

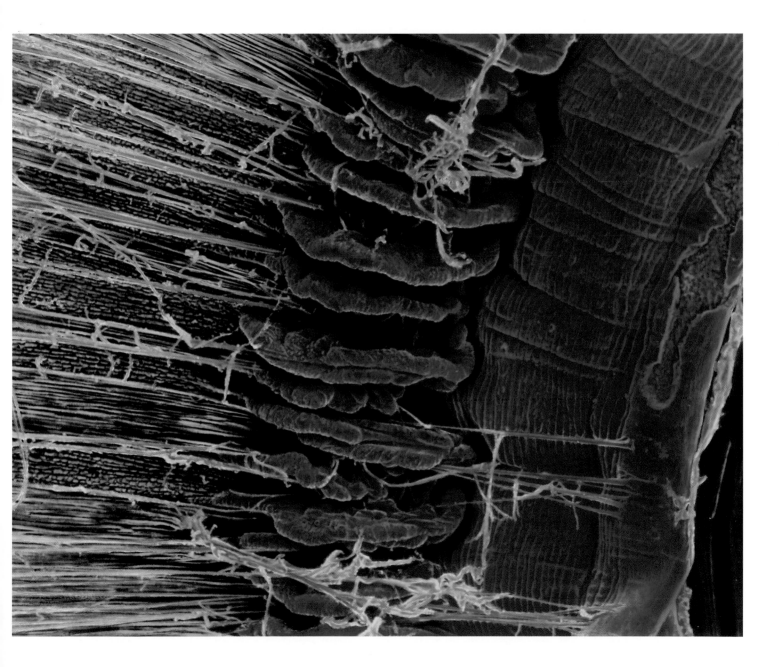

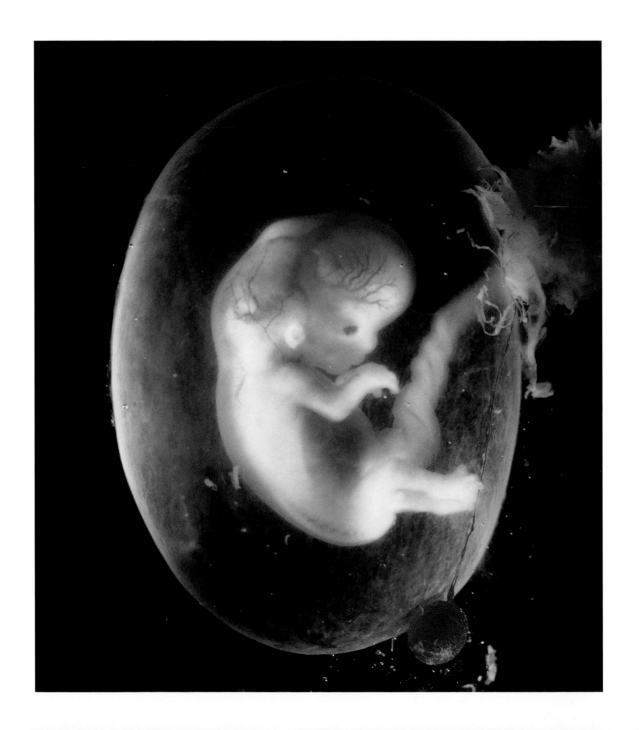

If biologists have ignored self-organization, it is not
because self-ordering is not pervasive and profound. It is because
we biologists have yet to understand how to think about systems governed
simultaneously by two sources of order, yet who seeing the snowflake, who seeing
simple lipid molecules cast adrift in water forming themselves into cell-like hollow lipid vesicles,
who seeing the potential for the crystallization of life in swarms of reacting molecules, who seeing
the stunning order for free in networks linking tens upon tens of thousands of variables, can fail
to entertain a central thought: if ever we are to attain a final theory in biology, we will
surely, surely have to understand the commingling of self-organization and selection.
We will have to see that we are the natural expressions of a deeper order.
Ultimately, we will discover in our creation myth that
we are expected after all.

STUART KAUFFMAN
At Home in the Universe

Human Embryo—*This is a view of a human embryo at 7-8 weeks old, attached to the
placenta and the mother's blood circulation by an umbilical cord. The embryo is seen floating
in an amniotic sac filled with amniotic fluid. At upper right is the remnant of the yolk sac. The
embryo's eye and limbs are visible, as is its male sex. At this age the embryo is about
4 centimeters in length and less than 10 grams in weight.*

The same stream of life that runs through my veins night and day
runs through the world and dances in rhythmic measures. It is the
same life that shoots in joy through the dust of the earth in number-
less blades of grass and breaks into tumultuous waves of leaves and
flowers. It is the same life that is rocked in the ocean-cradle of birth
and of death, in ebb and in flow. I feel my limbs are made glorious by
the touch of this world of life. And my pride is from the life-throb
of ages dancing in my blood this moment.

◦⊰ RABINDRANATH TAGORE ⊱◦
Gitanjali

Leafy Sea Dragon—*The leafy
sea dragon (Phycodurus equus) is unique to the
southern waters of Western Australia and Southern
Australia. The outer skin, or "hide," of the sea dragon is solid,
limiting its mobility, and the only way it can propel itself along is
through rapidly oscillating its ventral and dorsal fins. An extraordinary
feature of the leafy sea dragon is that it is actually the male of the
species which gets "pregnant and gives birth". During each breeding season, male leafy sea dragons will hatch two batches of about 100–250 eggs.*

This is my simple religion. There is no need for temples; no need for complicated philosophy. Our own brain, our own heart is our temple: the philosophy is kindness.

⌐ THE DALAI LAMA

Neuromuscular Junction—*At a neuromuscular junction, a motor neuron (pink) terminates on skeletal muscle fibers. The axon of a motor neuron terminates in several branching fibers, each of which ends in a cluster of small swellings, or boutons. When activated, the boutons release neurotransmitter chemicals from small vesicles, which diffuse across the gap (the synapse) separating the cells to interact with receptors in the muscle cell.*

Synapse—*This is a synapse, or junction, between two neurons in the human cerebral cortex, the outer gray matter of the brain. The synaptic gap (center) appears deep red. Information is conducted along nerves by a series of electrical impulses and from one nerve to another through the release of neurotransmitter chemicals which diffuse across the synaptic gap to trigger an electrical impulse in the neighboring nerve. Vesicles containing neurotransmitters are seen above the gap as small red/yellow spheres. The two large circular organelles (top) are mitochondria, the sites of energy production in the nerve cell.*

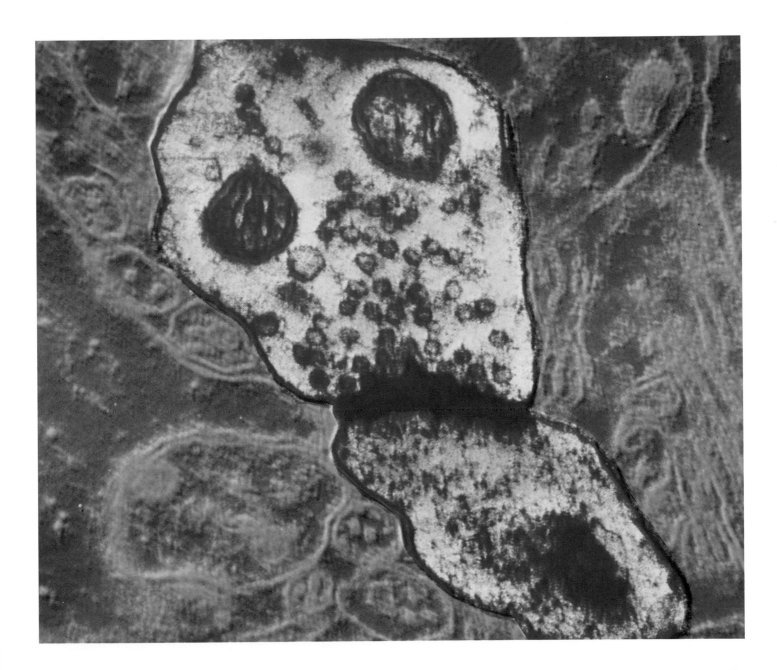

Every great advance in science has issued from
a new audacity of imagination.

❧ JOHN DEWEY ☙
The Quest for Certainty

Faith has to do with things that are not seen,
and hope with things that are not in hand.

❧ SAINT THOMAS AQUINAS ☙

Alpha-Endorphin—*Endorphins belong to a class of biochemicals commonly referred to as neurohormones that act by modifying the way in which nerve cells respond to transmitters. Four groups of endorphins, alpha, beta, gamma, and sigma, have so far been identified. Alpha-endorphin contains 16 amino acids, beta-endorphin contains 31 amino acids, gamma-endorphin contains 17, and sigma-endorphin has 27. Yet it is not the number of amino acids in an endorphin that determines its function; it is their order. The alpha-endorphin has only one less amino acid residue than the gamma-endorphin, yet the difference is profound. The alpha endorphin induces behavior similar to the stimulant amphetamine whereas the gamma-endorphin has strong links to the psychological condition schizophrenia.*

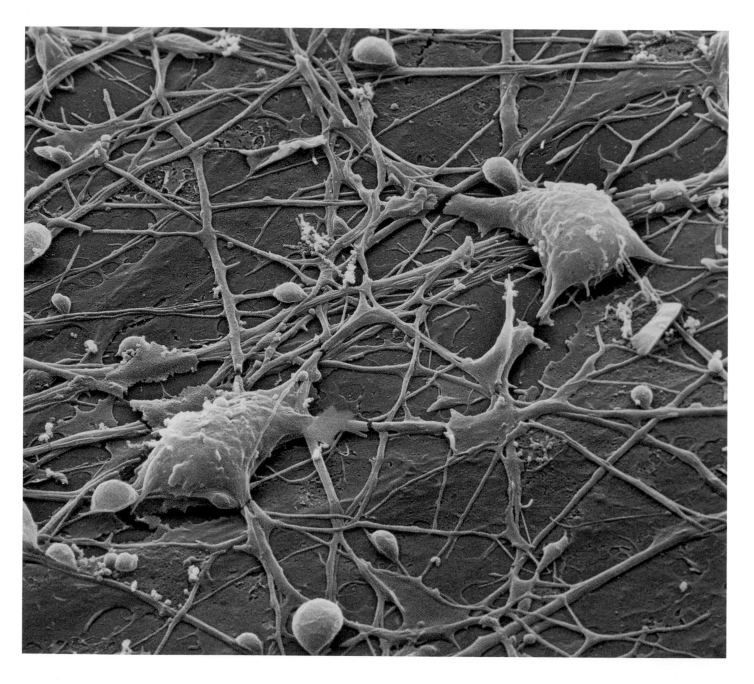

Despite many assertions to the contrary, the brain is not "like a computer."
Yes, the brain has many electrical connections, just like a computer. But at each
point in a computer only a binary decision can be made—yes or no, on or off, zero
or one. Each point in the brain, each brain cell, contains all the genetic information
necessary to reproduce the entire organism. A brain cell is not a switch. It has
a memory; it can be subtle. Each brain cell is like a computer. The brain is like
a hundred billion computers all connected together. It is impossible to understand
because it is too complex. As Emerson Pugh wrote, "If the human brain was
so simple that we could understand it, we would be so simple that we couldn't."

JEAN M. GOODWIN

Impossibility in Medicine: The Nature of the Impossible

Nerve cells, or neurons *(light brown),
typically consist of a cell body (lower left, upper
right) with several long processes extending from it. These
generally consist of one large axon (thick process) and several
dendrites (thinner). In a living system, the dendrites collect information, which is interpreted by the cell body and passed on along the
axon. Neurons allow information to be rapidly relayed around the body.*

Spiritual experiences are so consistent across cultures, across time, and across faiths that it suggests a common core that is likely a reflection of structures and processes in the human brain.

DAVID WULFF
Psychologist

For all the tentative successes that scientists are scoring in their search for the biological bases of religious, spiritual and mystical experience, one mystery will surely lie forever beyond their grasp. They may trace a sense of transcendence to *this* bulge on our gray matter. And they may trace a feeling of the devine to *that* one. But it is likely that they will never resolve the greatest question of all—namely, whether our brain wiring creates God, or whether God created our brain wiring. Which you believe is, in the end, a matter of faith.

SHARON BEGLEY
"Religion and the Brain," *Newsweek*

Tensor Map of the Brain—*Tensor maps can be used to visualize striking differences in the gyral patterns of the cerebral cortex. The complex patterns of anatomical variation shown in this map distinguish regions of high variability from areas of low variability. This map is based on a group of 20 elderly normal subjects. The resulting information can be leveraged to distinguish normal from abnormal anatomical variants using random tensor field algorithms.*

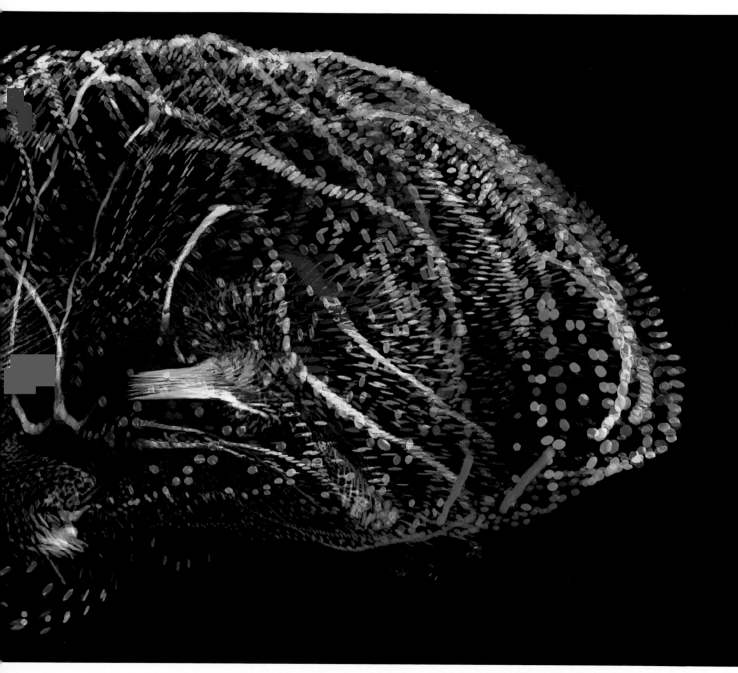

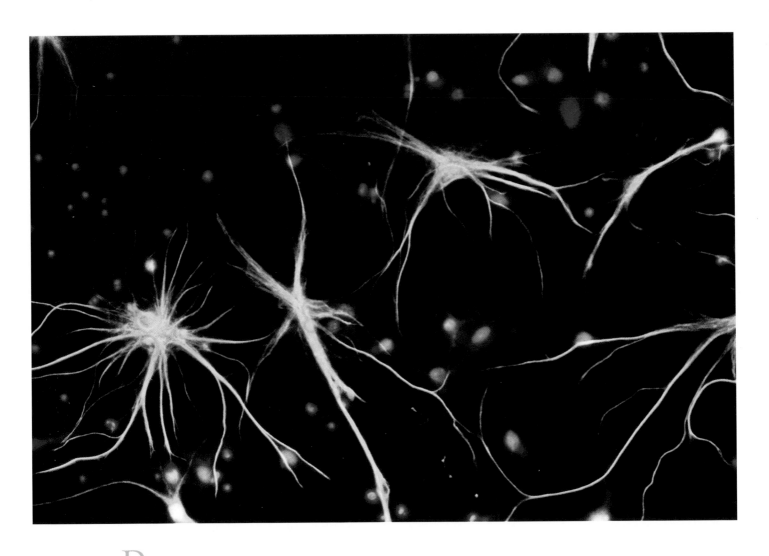

Philosophy itself cannot but benefit from our disputes, for if our conceptions prove true, new achievements will be made; if false, their refutation will further confirm the original doctrines.

GALILEO

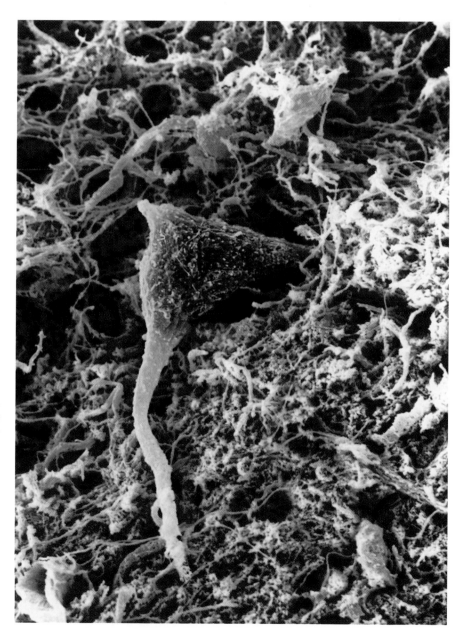

That's why religion thrives in an age of reason. You can't simply *think* God out of existence, because religious feelings rise more from *experience* than from thought. They are born in a moment of spiritual connection, as real to the brain as any perception of "ordinary" physical reality.

ANDREW NEWBERG
Neurotheologist, co-author,
Why God Won't Go Away

Neuron Cells and Astrocytes in Mammalian Spinal Cord— *Here neuron cells stain red: the cell body appears pink, with nerve fibers faintly seen which are the route of transmission of nerve impulses. In the foreground are astrocyte cells (green)—star-shaped connective tissue cells which provide support and nutrients for the neurons. It is thought that astrocytes may take part in information storage. Blue dots are the nuclei of other support cells.*

Nerve Cell—*A section of the gray matter in the brain showing a nerve cell (neuron), which consists of a cell body (upper center) with an axon nerve process or fiber seen leading off it to lower frame. The axon transmits nerve impulses away from the cell body. This nerve cell is embedded in gray matter (yellow) made up of branched dendrite nerve fibers, small support cells, and other nerve cells. Dendrites transmit impulses from other nerve cells to this cell body, thereby communicating with this nerve cell. Gray matter in the cortex of the cerebrum of the brain is involved in conscious thought and memory.*

Four stages of acceptance:
1) this is worthless nonsense;
2) this is an interesting, but perverse, point of view;
3) this is true, but quite unimportant;
4) I always said so.

J. B. S. HALDANE
Journal of Genetics

Cybernetic Circuitry—*This neuron, on a silicon chip, is immobilized between polyimide pillars. The cell was cultured on the circuit until it formed a network with nearby neurons (for example, far left). Under each cell is a transistor, which can excite the neuron above it. The neuron then passes a signal to the neurons attached to it, which activates the transistors beneath them. This experiment shows that hybrid neuron-silicon circuits are feasible.*

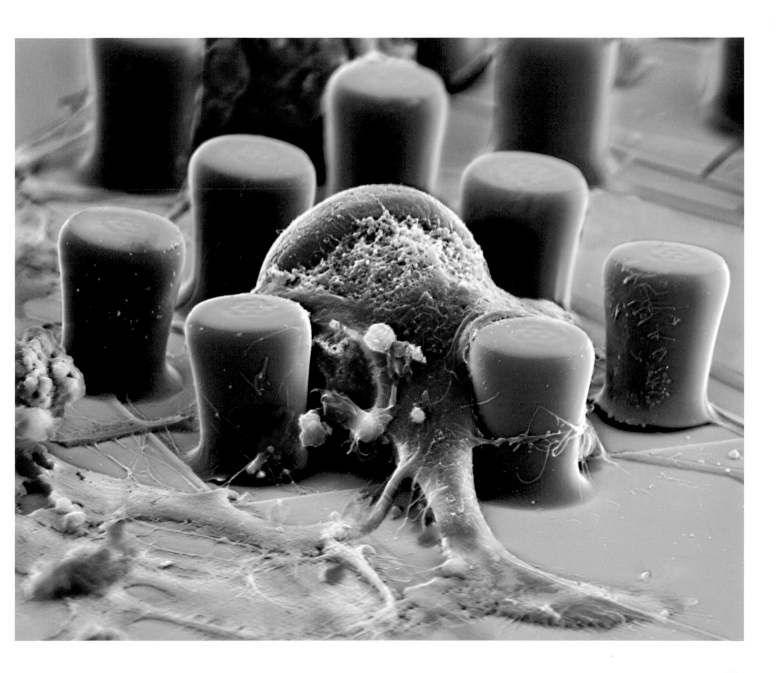

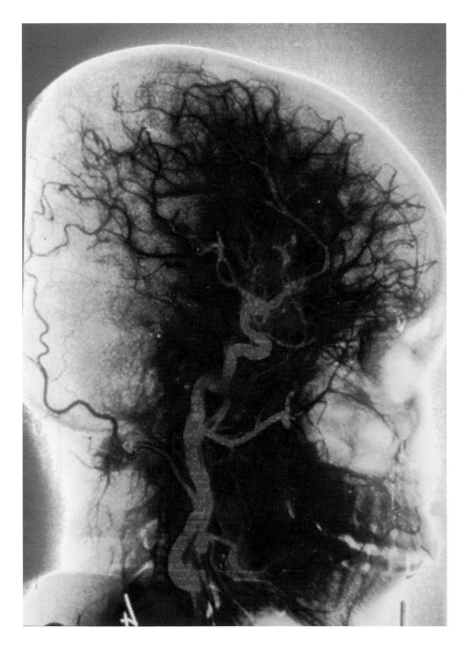

The universe is not rough-hewn, but perfect in its details. Nature will bear the closest inspection; she invites us to lay our eye level with the smallest leaf, and take an insect view of its plain. She has no interstices; every part is full of life.

⌐ HENRY DAVID THOREAU
American philosopher, author, naturalist

Science is wonderfully equipped to answer the question "How?" but it gets terribly confused when you ask the question "Why?"

⌐ ERWIN CHARGAFF

Human Head—*This is a hi-tech, color-digitized angiogram of a human head. An angiogram is an x-ray, or roentgenogram, of a vessel obtained by outlining the structure with a radiopaque material. The largest vessel near the base of the skull is the internal carotid artery.*

My commonsense interpretation of the facts suggests that a super-intellect has monkeyed with physics, as well as with chemistry and biology, and that there are no blind forces worth speaking about in nature. The numbers one calculates from the facts seem to me so overwhelming as to put this conclusion almost beyond question.

SIR FRED HOYLE
British mathematician, astronomer, and cosmologist

Adrenaline—*These are crystals of adrenaline (epinephrine), a hormone produced in the adrenal glands above the kidneys. Adrenaline is normally present in blood in small quantities. However, in times of stress large quantities are secreted into the bloodstream. Adrenaline widens the airways of the lungs, constricts small blood vessels, and liberates sugar stored in the liver. This makes the muscles work harder and produce a "fight or flight" response. Adrenaline used as a drug expands the bronchioles in acute asthma attacks or stimulates the heart in cases of anaphylactic shock.*

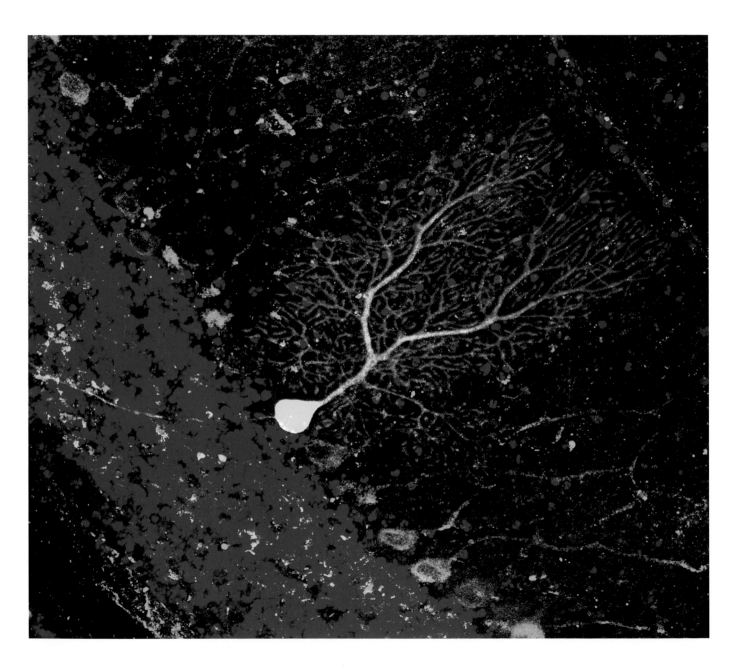

After all, the ultimate goal of all research is not objectivity, but truth.

❡ HELENE DEUTSCH
The Psychology of Women

Man will occasionally stumble over the truth, but usually manages to pick himself up, walk over or around it, and carry on.

❡ WINSTON CHURCHILL

Purkinje Nerve Cell—*This is a section through a Purkinje nerve cell (yellow/orange) from the cerebellum of the brain. The Purkinje cell comprises a flask-shaped cell body (yellow) from which branch numerous dendrites (orange). Purkinje cells are found at the junction between the granular layer (blue, lower left) and the molecular layer (green) of the gray matter of the cerebellum. Nerve impulses flow to a Purkinje cell through its dendrites. The cerebellum controls balance, posture and muscle coordination.*

Transmitting Neuron—*A transmitting neuron transmits the nerve impulses. There are over 28 billion neurons in the human body. A longitudinal section through the nerve illustrates some very important structures to this nerve. The indentation is the node of ranvier. This node stimulates the neural signal and gives it a boost.*

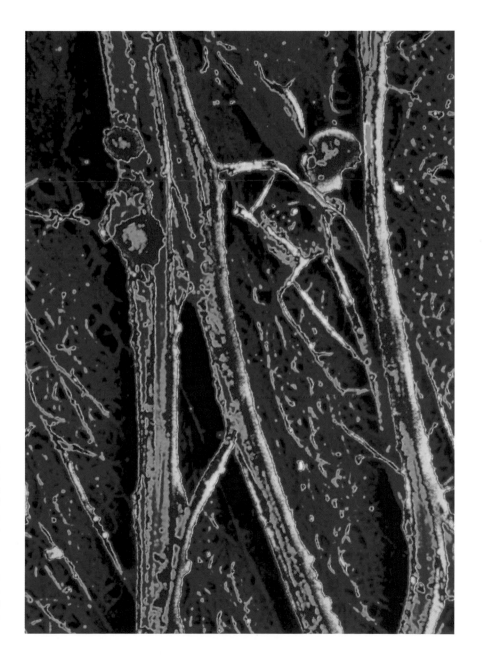

What the caterpillar calls the end of the world
the master calls a butterfly.

❧ RICHARD BACH ❧
Illusions

In spite of the fact that religion looks backward to revealed truth
while science looks forward to new vistas and discoveries, both
activities produce a sense of awe and a curious mixture of humility
and arrogance in practitioners. All great scientists are inspired by
the subtlety and beauty of the natural world that they are seeking
to understand. Each new subatomic particle, every unexpected object,
produces delight and wonderment. In constructing their theories,
physicists are frequently guided by arcane concepts of elegance in
the belief that the universe is intrinsically beautiful.

❧ PAUL DAVIES ❧
God and the New Physics

Cortisol, or Hydro-
Cortisone, *is the chief steroid hormone*
secreted by the adrenal cortex. Cortisol plays a role in
both normal carbohydrate metabolism and in the body's
response to physical and emotional stress. Although its short-term
effects are exerted in conjunction with the adrenaline hormones, longer
lasting actions are exerted independently and relate to adaptation of the
body to improve defense against infection to promote tissue repair, and provide
adequate nutrients in the form of glucose and amino acids. Cortisol is used
medically to treat inflammation arising from injury, allergies, and rheumatoid disorders.

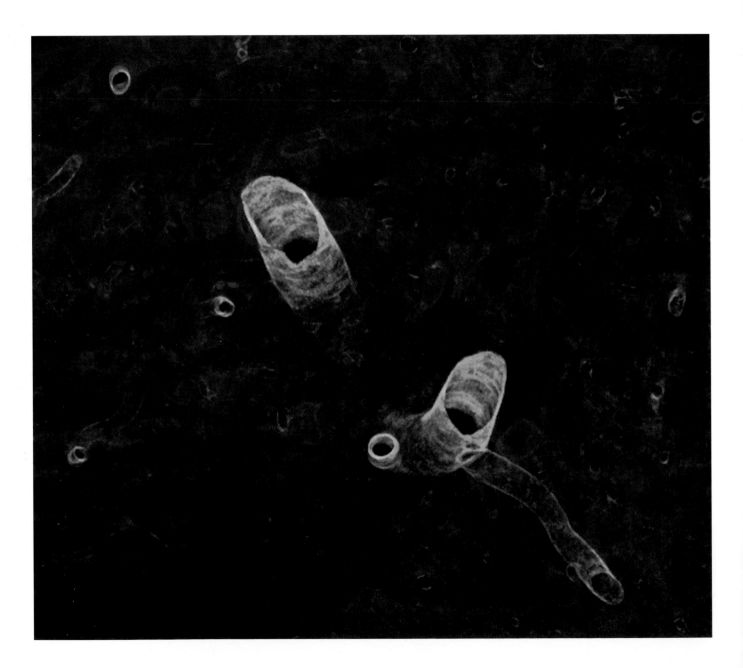

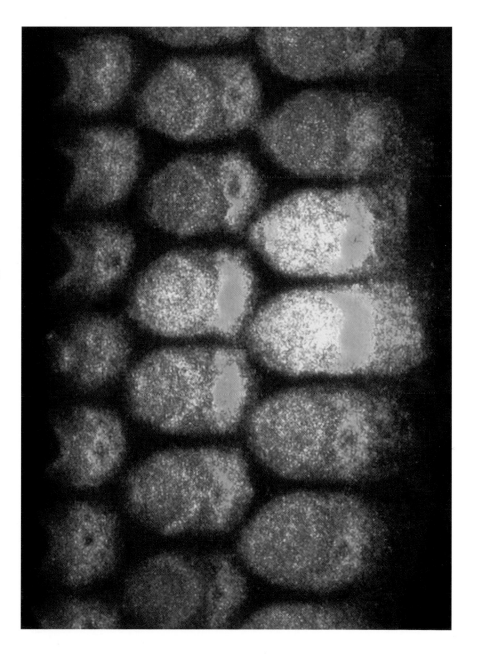

Science is not the affirmation of a set of beliefs but a process of inquiry aimed at building a testable body of knowledge constantly open to rejection or confirmation. In science, knowledge is fluid and certainty fleeting. That is at the heart of its limitations. It is also its greatest strength.

MICHAEL SHERMER
Why People Believe Weird Things

Blood Vessels in the Brainstem—*The green tube-like structures are small arteries called arterioles that run through the brainstem. Cells called pericytes, which act as support cells for the blood vessel walls, are stained red. When these cells are activated, as they are here, they appear to have the ability to filter out unwanted material from the bloodstream.*

Inner Ear Hair Cells—*The V-shaped rows of hair cells (bright arcs) in the organ of Corti, lie in the cochlea of the inner ear, and convert sound vibrations into nerve impulses. The hairs (stereocilia) are embedded in the basilar membrane. When sound waves arrive at this membrane from the middle ear, they cause it to vibrate. This pushes the hair cells against the overlying tectorial membrane (not seen). This triggers nerve impulses, which travel to the brain through the auditory nerve.*

Our time is a time of the ascendancy of ethics, because cutting edge science means that we can do more. The question then becomes: Ought we do what we can do? You always have the ascendancy of moral and ethical issues when you have a new range of possibilities.

of LARRY L. RASMUSSEN ⅝
Professor of Social Ethics
Union Theological Seminary

There's no single magic bullet . . . But I think that stem cells will lead the way if we want to get rid of these diseases. If we want to ease the suffering of millions, we now have a new tool, and we should just thank God for it.

of CHRISTOPHER REEVE ⅝
Actor, advocate of stem cell research

And yet God's law protects us from our own follies. If stem cells are to be a God-given means to enhance and preserve human life, can we not search for these means in accord with His will?

of FR. DANIEL NASSANEY ⅝
Director, Immaculata Retreat House

Stem Cells—*Stem cells, taken from umbilical cord blood, are known as multipotent because they undergo differentiation to produce precursors of all the body's specialized blood cells. By this process, termed haemopoiesis, stem cells develop into either red blood cells or one of several types of white blood cells that make up the immune system. The purification of stem cells from umbilical cord blood allows scientists to research the function of the immune system and to develop treatments for diseases such as AIDS and leukemia.*

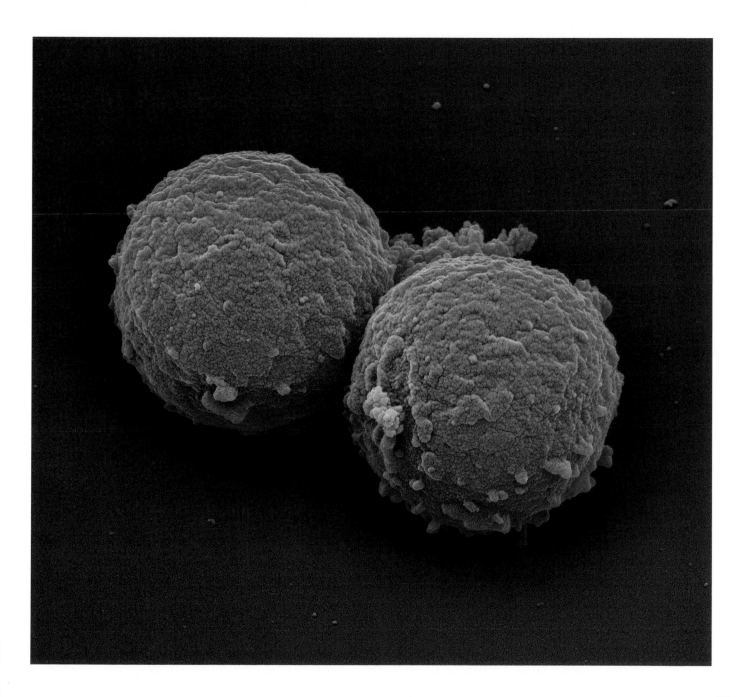

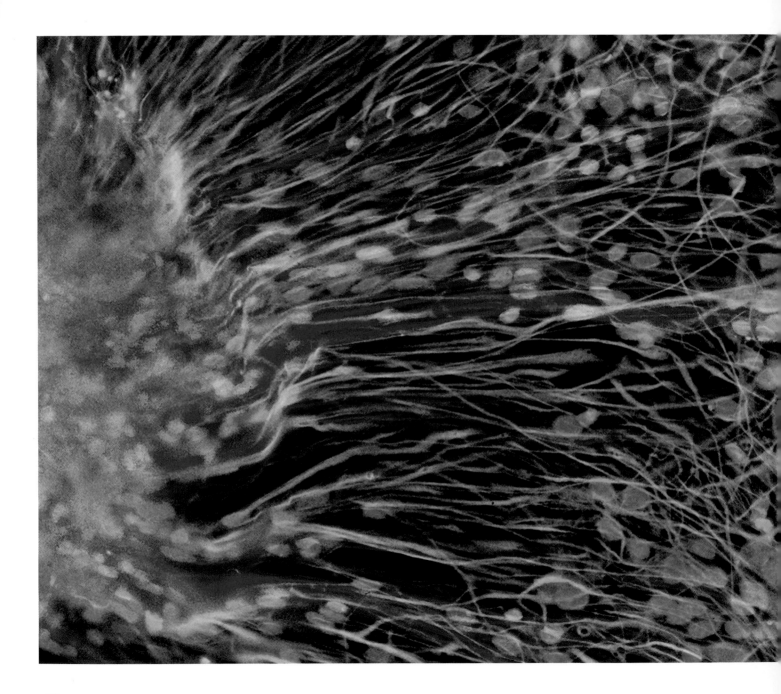

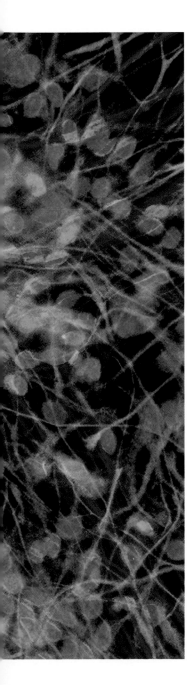

Even though the realms of religion and science in themselves are clearly marked off from each other, nevertheless there exist between the two strong reciprocal relationships and dependencies. Though religion may be that which determines the goal, it has, nevertheless, learned from science, in the broadest sense, what means will contribute to the attainment of the goals it has set up. But science can only be created by those who are thoroughly imbued with an aspiration towards truth and understanding. The source of feeling, however, springs from the sphere of religion. To this there also belongs the faith in the possibility that the regulations valid for the world of existence are rational, that is, comprehensible to reason. I cannot conceive of a genuine scientist without that profound faith. The situation may be expressed by an image: Science without religion is lame, religion without science is blind.

ALBERT EINSTEIN
Out of My Later Years

Embryonic Stem Cells—*This image depicts cells derived from human embryonic stem cells. Precursor neural cells grow in a lab dish and generate mature neurons (red) and glial cells (green).*

Religion is a wizard a sibyl...
She faces the wreck of worlds,
and prophesies restoration.
She faces a sky blood-red with
sunset colors that deepen into darkness,
and prophesies dawn.
She faces death,
and prophesies life.

FELIX ALDER
Founder of the Ethical Culture Movement, 1876

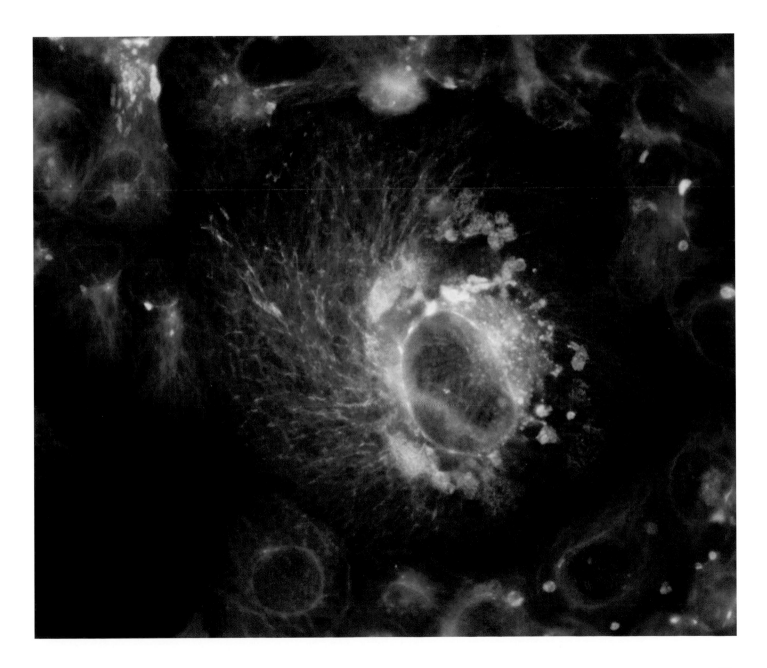

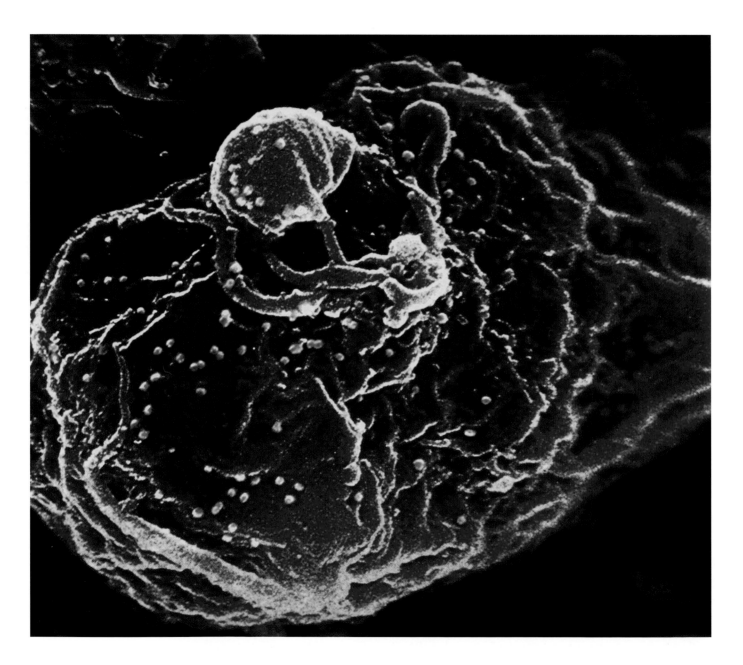

I saw things there—what we would call miraculous healings—
that didn't fit with what I was taught in medical school,
but the Africans had faith because they had never been
taught such things were impossible. I learned that you
don't have to see to believe. You have to believe to see.

DR. DAVE HILTON
Emory University Chaplain

AIDS Virus—In this HIV-1
infected T4 lymphocyte the virus can be seen
budding from the membrane. The first report of
AIDS came in June of 1981, when the CDC published a
report about the occurrence, without identifiable cause, of
Pneumocystis carinii pneumonia (PCP) in five men in Los Angeles.

Science can purify religion from error and superstition. Religion can purify science from idolatry and false absolutes.

✢ POPE JOHN PAUL II

The extravagant gesture is the very stuff of creation. After one extravagant gesture of creation in the first place, the universe has continued to deal exclusively in extravagances, flinging intricacies and colossi down aeons of emptiness, heaping profusions on profligacies with fresh vigor. The whole show has been on fire since the word go!

✢ ANNIE DILLARD
Pilgrim at Tinker Creek

Crixivan *is an anti-retroviral drug that acts as a protease inhibitor and is effective in combating HIV replication in patients afflicted with AIDS. Drugs of this type disrupt the production of protein products necessary to produce infective HIV virons, thus dramatically reducing the number of infectious particles in the body.*

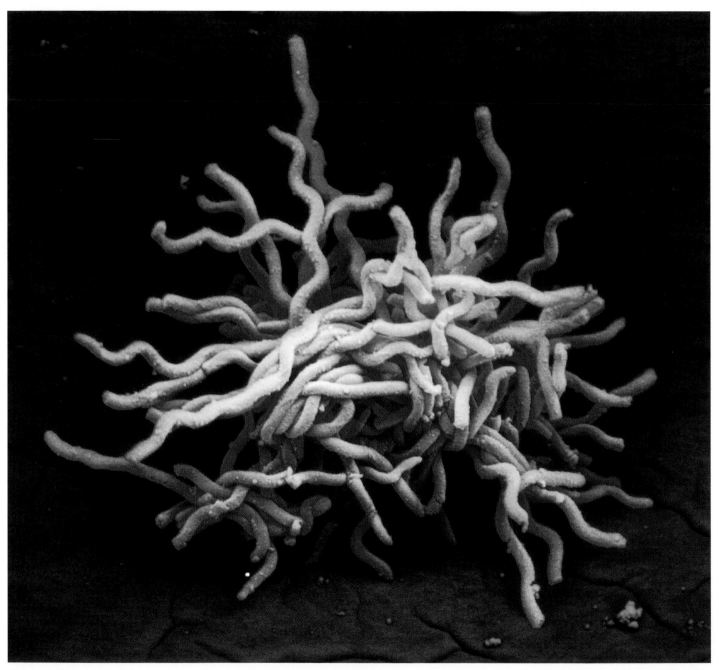

And almost every one when age,
Disease, or sorrows strike him,
Inclines to think there is a God,
Or something very like Him.

⌐ ARTHUR HUGH CLOUGH
   Anglo-American poet

Whatever evil voices may rage,
science, secure among the powers
that are eternal, will do her work
and be blessed.

⌐ THOMAS HENRY HUXLEY
   Aphorisms and Reflections

Lyme Disease Bacteria—*These spiral-shaped spirochaete bacteria, colored yellow, are a conglomeration of Borrelia burgdorferi bacteria, the cause of Lyme disease in humans. They are passed on to humans by tick bites, which can infest domestic dogs. Symptoms of Lyme disease include skin lesions, muscle pain, neurological and cardiac abnormalities, and arthritis.*

Hodgkin's Disease *is a cancer of the lymphoreticular system —the mediator of non-specific cell defense mechanisms and the immune response. The various cell lines of the system are all subject to cancerous changes. In Hodgkin's disease, the nature of the cell line is unknown, but in the most common form the cell population is mixed.*

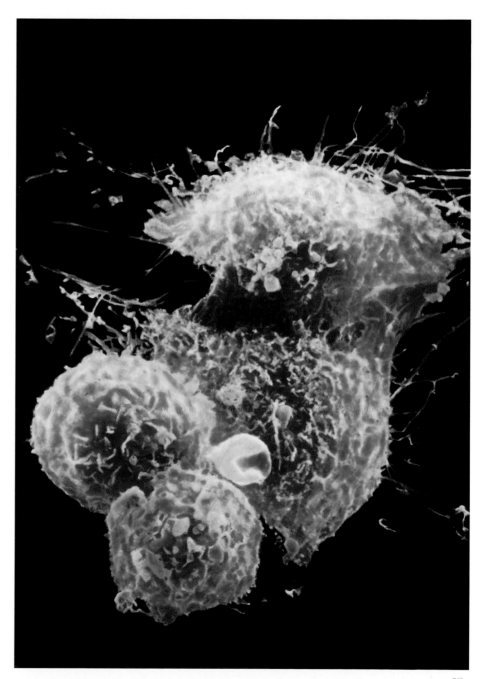

Science tries to answer the question: "How?" How do cells act in the body? How do you design an airplane that will fly faster than sound? How is a molecule of insulin constructed? Religion, by contrast, tries to answer the question: "Why?" Why was man created? Why ought I to tell the truth? Why must there be sorrow or pain or death? Science attempts to analyze how things and people and animals behave; it has no concern whether this behavior is good or bad, is purposeful or not. But religion is precisely the quest for such answers: whether an act is right or wrong, good or bad, and why.

WARREN WEAVER
Science and Imagination

Lung Cancer—*This is a small cancerous tumor (blue) filling an alveolus of the human lung. Alveoli are the blind-ended air sacs which make up the lungs. Here, the individual cancer cells are coated with microscopic, hair-like structures known as microvilli. A number of cancer cells can also be seen separated from the main tumor. The most common cause of lung cancer is cigarette smoking.*

89

Faith and doubt both are needed, not as antagonists,
but working side by side to take us around
the unknown curve.

   LILLIAN SMITH
     American novelist, educator

Here is the test to find whether your mission on earth
is finished. If you're alive, it isn't.

   RICHARD BACH
     Author

Taxol—*In December 1992 the FDA approved Taxol for refractory ovarian cancer. Today it is used
for a variety of cancers, including ovarian, breast, non-small-cell lung, and Karposi's sarcoma. The
drug is being tested against a variety of other cancers. Originally, the only source of Taxol was the
Pacific yew; to treat one patient required the harvest of six, 100-year-old trees. Today, the drug
is made by a semi-synthetic process from Taxus baccata.*

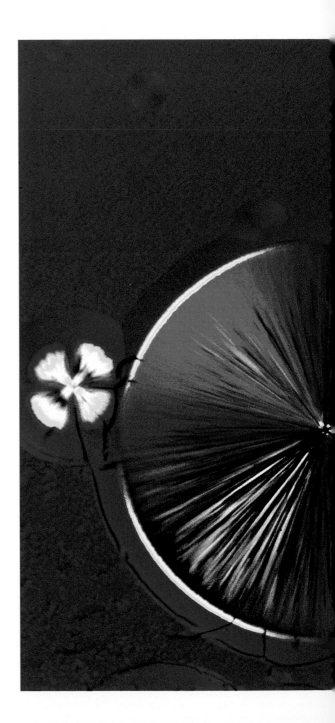

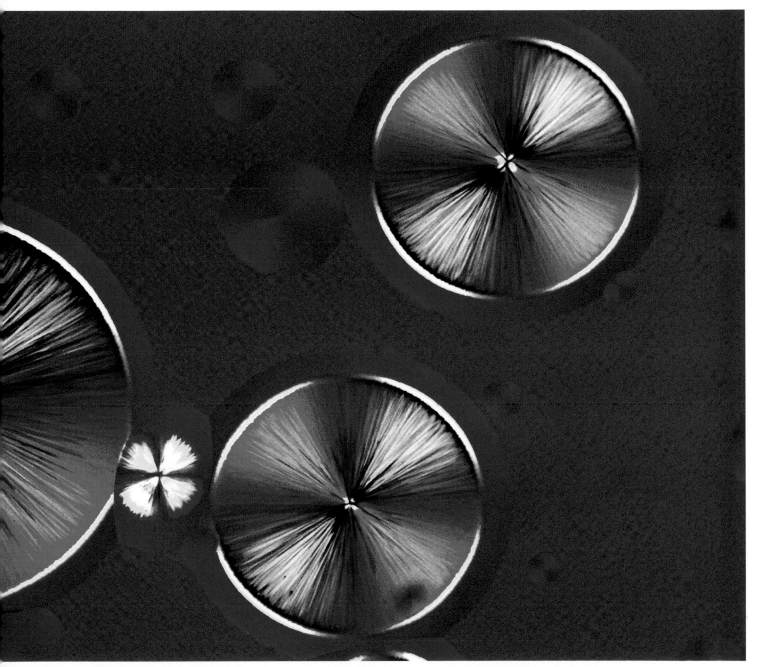

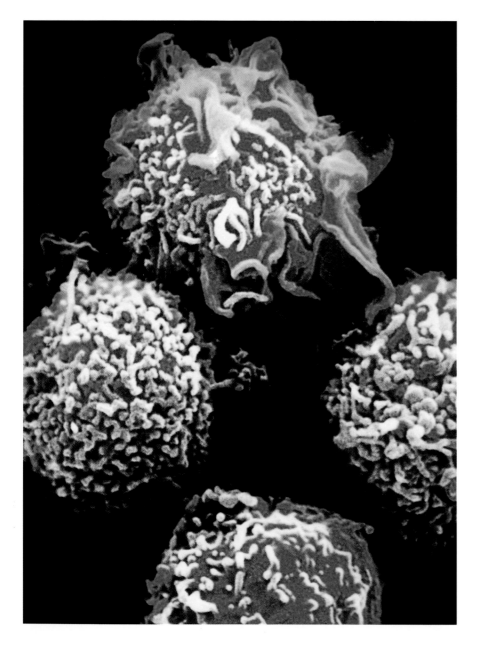

vil being the root of mystery,
pain is the root of knowledge.

SIMONE WEIL
French philosopher, mystic

Hairy-Cell Leukemia—*These abnormal white blood cells (B-lymphocytes) show characteristic hair-like cytoplasmic projections and ruffles on their surfaces, which can be found in patients suffering from hairy-cell leukemia. Leukemia is a blood cancer in which the blood-producing tissue in bone marrow produces excessive numbers of immature white blood cells, as seen here, which impair the function of normal blood cells. The immune system is thus weakened. Hairy cell leukemia is a rare form of leukemia that affects mostly men. Most patients survive for five years or more after diagnosis.*

Colon Cancer—*These goblet cells (three holes) on the mucosal surface of a cancerous colon have numerous microvilli (hair-like projections) covering the whole surface. These absorb nutrients and secrete digestive substances. The goblet cells secrete the mucus that lines the intestinal tract. Cancer is the abnormal proliferation of malignant cells, and colon cancer is one of the most common cancers in the developed world.*

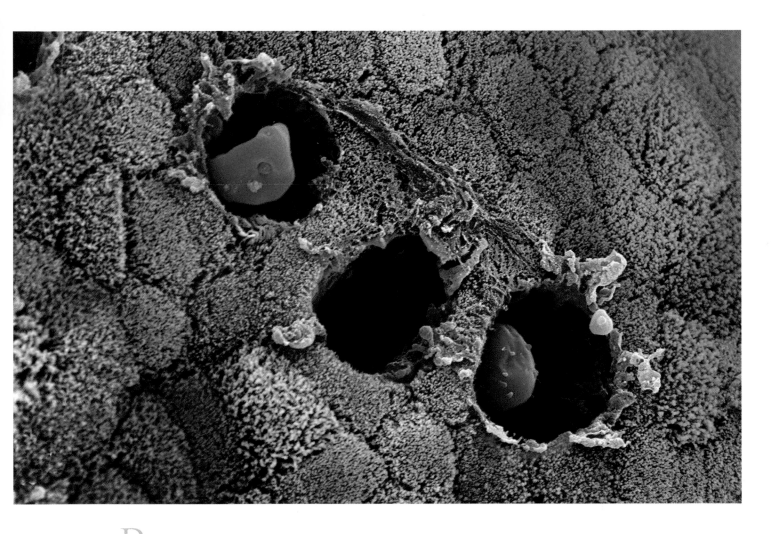

P̲eople are like stained-glass windows: they sparkle and shine when the sun is out, but when the darkness sets in their true beauty is revealed only if there is a light within.

❖   ELIZABETH KÜBLER-ROSS, M.D.   ❧
On Death and Dying

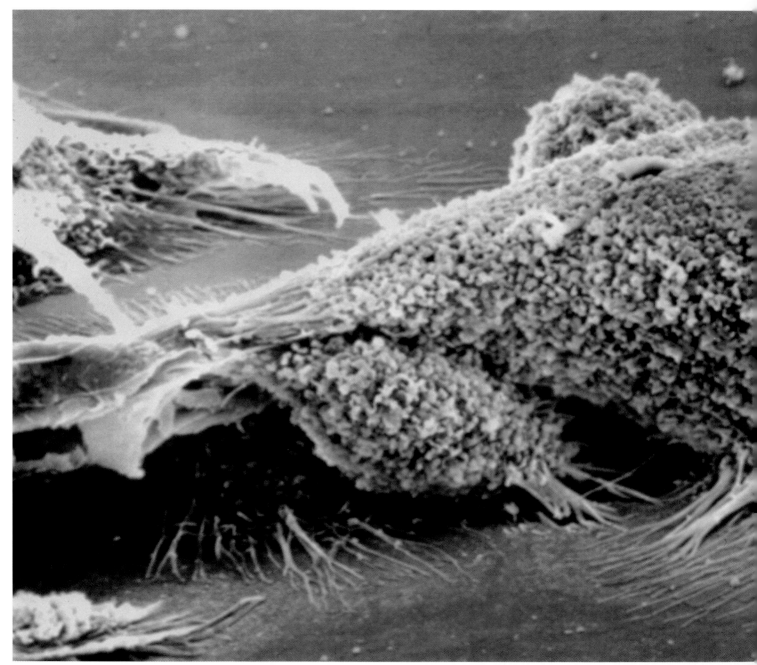

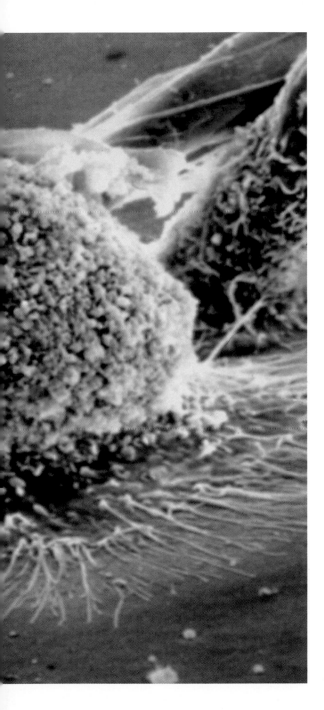

I know God won't give me anything I can't handle. I just wish He didn't trust me so much.

❧ MOTHER TERESA

The happiest excitement in life is to be convinced that one is fighting for all one is worth on behalf of some clearly seen and deeply felt good.

❧ RUTH BENEDICT
American anthropologist

Breast Cancer Cell—*Extra cells in the breast will form a mass of tissue called a growth or tumor. Cells in these tumors are abnormal. They divide without control or order, and they can invade and damage nearby tissues and organs. Other than skin cancer, breast cancer is the most common type of cancer among women in the United States. More than 180,000 women are diagnosed with breast cancer each year.*

Faith is believing in things when common sense tells you not to.

    ⌐ GEORGE SEATON
       Screenwriter, *Miracle On 34th Street*

Weave in faith and God will find the thread.

    ⌐ SCHOPENHAUER
       German philosopher

Faith is the substance of things hoped for, the evidence of things not seen.

    ⌐ HEBREWS 11:1

Adriamycin *is the common name for the drug doxorubicin hydrochloride that is thought to bind DNA and inhibit nucleic acid synthesis. The drug has been used to successfully produce regression in disseminated neoplastic situations. Examples are acute lymphoblastic leukemia, acute myeloblastic leukemia, Wilm's tumor, soft tissue and bone sarcomas, breast carcinoma, ovarian carcinoma and many other ailments.*

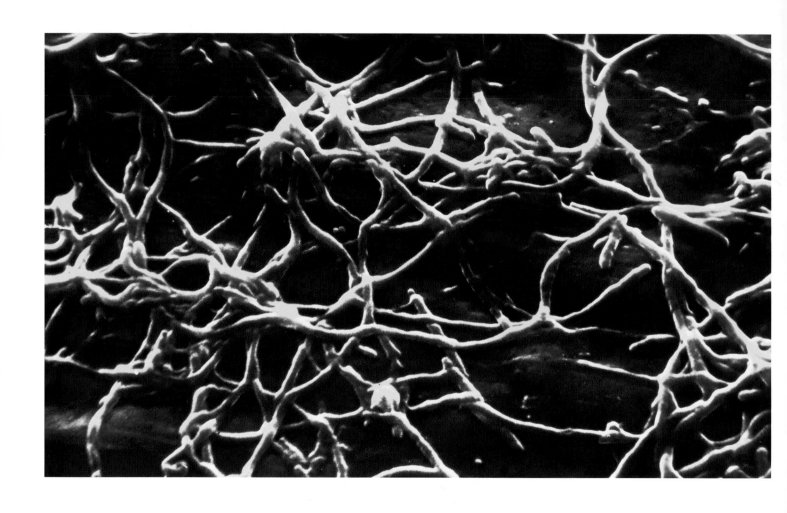

What is to give light must endure burning.

❧ VIKTOR FRANKL ☙
Author, neurologist, psychiatrist,
Holocaust survivor

Only those who will risk going too far can possibly find out how far one can go.

⌐ T.S. ELIOT
Poet, critic

We are not human beings on a spiritual journey. We are spiritual beings on a human journey.

⌐ STEPHEN COVEY
Author

Legionella Pneumophila—*This is a colony of* Legionella pneumophila, *the bacteria causing Legionnaires' disease, a severe and often fatal form of lobar pneumonia. The weakly staining gram negative bacterium is elongated with a single flagellum for motility. The disease obtained its name after an outbreak at an American Legion Convention in Pennsylvania in 1976.*

Cerebral Aneurysm—*Colored X-ray angiogram of a berry aneurysm (black, lower center) at the end of the internal carotid artery, which supplies the brain, eyes and forehead with blood. The big black vessel at the bottom is the internal carotid artery in the base of the brain. This branches in the middle of the picture into a network of smaller vessels (top) that feed the brain. Aneurysms are abnormal swellings in arteries caused by the pressure of blood flowing through a weakened area. Cerebral aneurysms are especially dangerous because they can rupture, causing a life-threatening brain hemorrhage with symptoms similar to stroke.*

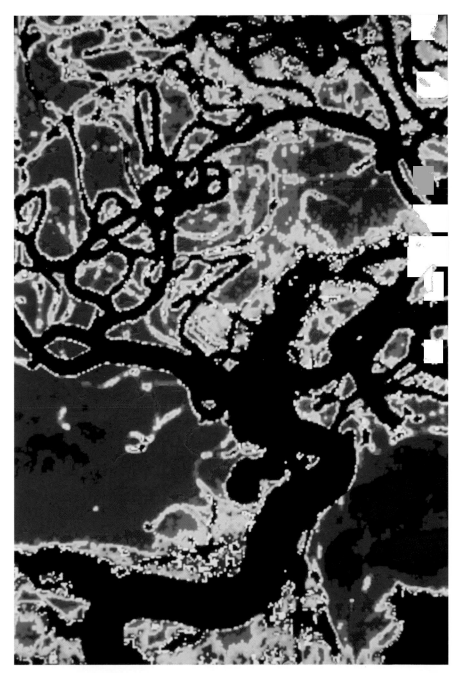

$\mathcal{S}$cience gives us the grounds of premises from which religious truths are to be inferred; but it does not set about inferring them, much less does it reach the inference; that is not its province. It brings before us phenomena, and it leaves us, if we will, to call them works of design, wisdom, or benevolence; and further still if we will, to proceed to confess an Intelligent Creator. We have to take its facts, and to give them a meaning, and to draw our own conclusions from them. First comes Knowledge, then a view, then reasoning, then belief. This is why Science has so little of a religious tendency; deductions have no power of persuasion. The heart is commonly reached, not through the reason, but through the imagination, by means of direct impressions, by the testimony of facts and events, by history, by description. Persons influence us, voices melt us, looks subdue us, deeds inflame us. Many a man will live and die upon a dogma; no man will be a martyr for a conclusion.

JOHN HENRY NEWMAN
British theologian,
Tamworth Reading Room, 1841

Alzheimer's Disease Culture Cell—*This cell, used in Alzheimer's disease research, has been genetically engineered to produce amyloid precursor protein (APP), which in turn forms the protein amyloid. Plaques of amyloid in the brain are a major pathological feature of Alzheimer's disease. This cell was cultured from a nerve cancer (neuroblastoma) and has shorter and more numerous processes (dendrites and axons) than a healthy nerve cell. Alzheimer's is a brain-wasting disease common in the elderly. It causes confusion, memory loss, personality changes, and eventually death.*

What is the meaning of human life, or of organic life altogether? To answer this question at all implies a religion. Is there any sense then, you ask, in putting it? I answer, the man who regards his own life and that of his fellow creatures as meaningless is not merely unfortunate but almost disqualified for life.

     ALBERT EINSTEIN
     The World as I See It

A man should use that spiritual heritage which he has received from the wise and holy people of the past, but he should test everything with his intellect, accepting certain things and rejecting others.

     LEO TOLSTOY
     A Calendar of Wisdom

Stroke—*This is a colored three-dimensional magnetic resonance angiogram (MRA) scan showing a human brain after a stroke, or cerebrovascular accident (CVA). Major arteries are white. The central region (yellow) is an area of bleeding, or hemorrhage. Stroke is brain damage caused by the interruption of the brain's blood supply or by the leakage of blood through blood vessel walls. The two main causes are high blood pressure and narrowing of the arteries due to fat deposition (atherosclerosis). Strokes vary in severity but can result in long-term paralysis, coma, and death.*

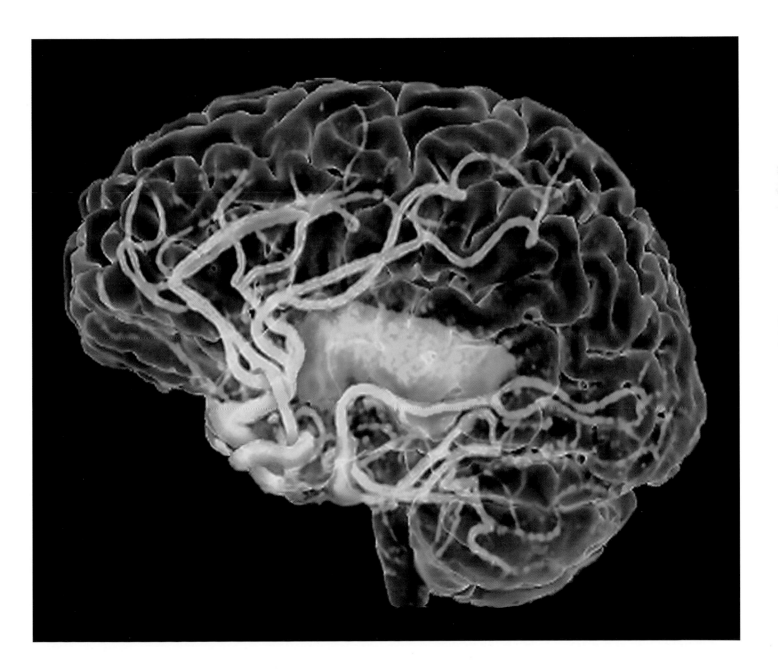

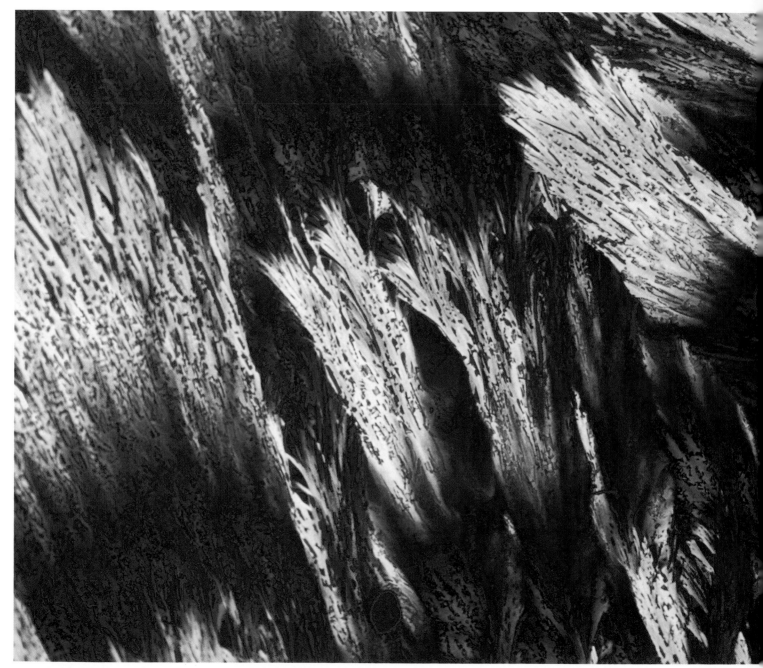

$\mathcal{S}$cience is not about control. It is about cultivating a perpetual condition of wonder in the face of something that forever grows one step richer and subtler than our latest theory about it. It is about reverence, not mastery.

RICHARD POWER
Dialogue from *The Goldberg Variations*

$\mathcal{W}$hat lies behind us and what lies before are tiny matters compared to what lies within us.

RALPH WALDO EMERSON

Norepinephrine—*The connection between the axons of one cell and the dendrites of an adjacent cell is called a synapse. The transmission of signals across a synapse is accomplished by the use of small chemical messengers that are termed neurotransmitters. There are several major classes of neurotransmitters that function in several types of synaptic junctions. Acetyl choline is used for fast responses, catecholamines transmit signals in adrenergic synapses of the brain and smooth muscle, whereas some amino acids act as neurotransmitters used in inhibitory signals.*

In conclusion, there is a marvelous anecdote from the occasion of Russell's 90th birthday that best serves to summarize his attitude toward God and religion. A London lady sat next to him at this party, and over the soup she suggested to him that he was not only the world's most famous atheist, but, by this time, very probably the world's oldest atheist. "What will you do, Bertie, if it turns out you're wrong?" she asked. "I mean, what if—uh—when the time comes, you should meet Him? What will you say?" Russell was delighted with the question. His bright, birdlike eyes grew even brighter as he contemplated this possible future dialogue, and then pointed a finger upward and cried, "Why, I should say, 'God, you gave us insufficient evidence.'"

AL SECKEL
Preface to
Bertrand Russell on God and Religion

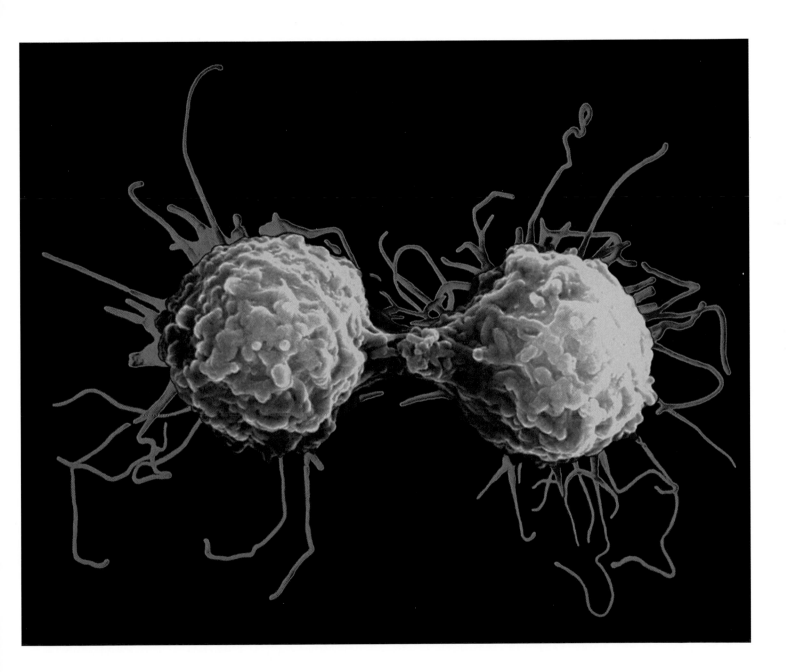

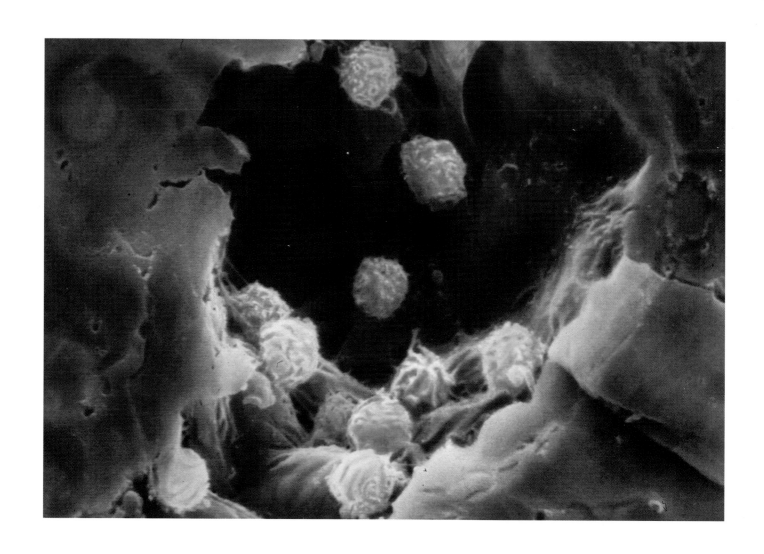

Don't pray when it rains, if you don't pray when the sun shines.

❧ LEROY [SATCHEL] PAIGE ☙
American baseball player

We do not believe in immortality because we can prove it, but we try to prove it because we cannot help believing it.

⌐ HARRIET MARTINEAU

God is like a mirror. The mirror never changes, but everybody who looks at it sees something different.

⌐ RABBI HAROLD KUSHNER

Lymphocyte in a Venule—*A lymphocyte is a white blood cell that is formed in lymphoid tissue. A venule is a vein that is usually less than 100 um in diameter. Endothelial cells line blood vessels.*

Macrophage *attached to an endothelial cell, with lymphocyte attached. A macrophage is a large mononuclear cell which ingests degenerated cells and blood tissue. A lymphocyte is a white blood cell. Endothelial cells make up the endothelium, the tissue of blood vessels.*

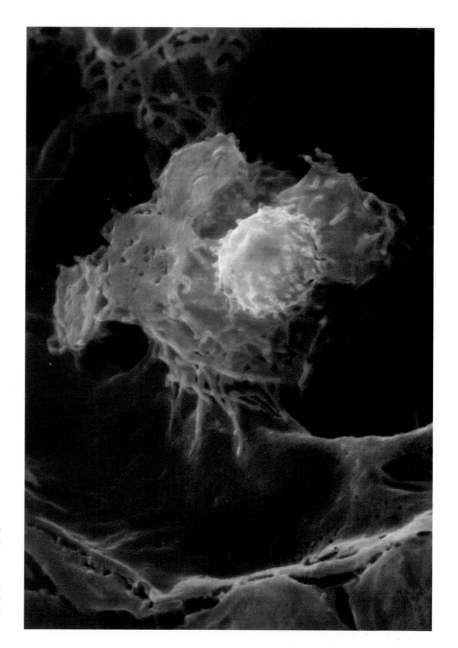

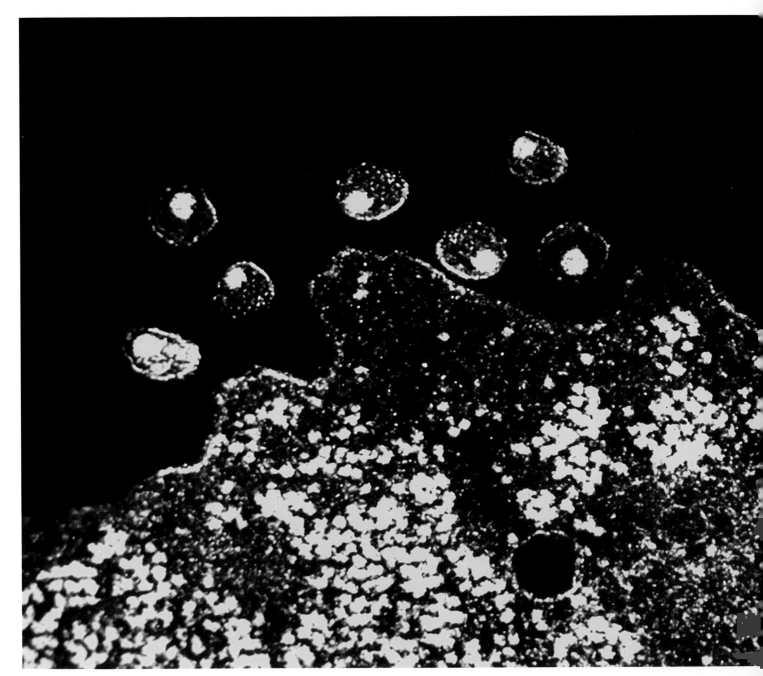

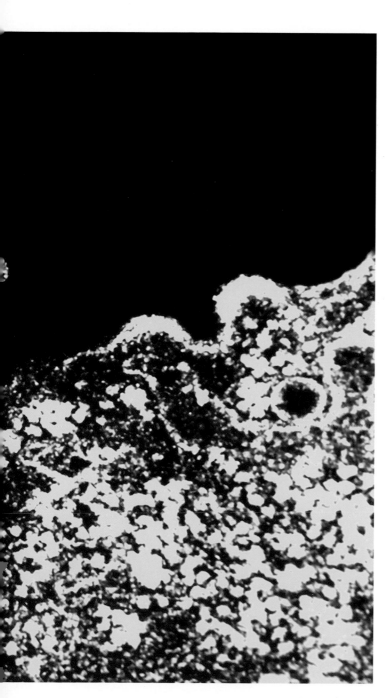

Many have not been told that birth into a physical world is a death in the spiritual worlds from which they came. Hence most are never aware that death in the physical world is merely a birth into other dimensions of life.

◫ JESSE HOLMES

Illness is not something a person has. It's another way of being.

◫ JONATHAN MILLER
The Body in Question

AIDS Virus—*This image shows mature virus and immature viruses budding from a lymphocyte. AIDS is a chronic, life-threatening condition caused by the human immunodeficiency virus (HIV). By damaging or destroying the cells of the immune system, HIV interferes with the body's ability to effectively fight off viruses, bacteria, and fungi that cause disease. This makes one more susceptible to opportunistic infections the body would normally resist, such as pneumonia and meningitis, and to certain types of cancers.*

I am careful not to confuse excellence with perfection. Excellence, I can reach for; perfection is God's business.

⌐ MICHAEL J. FOX
Quoted in Lorne A. Adrain's
The Most Important Thing I Know

Mistakes are the portals of discovery.

⌐ JAMES JOYCE
Ulysses

Dideoxyinosine (DDI, Didanosine)—*Didanosine, an anti-AIDS drug that seems to help, is marketed in the United States and Canada under the trade name Videx. This nucleotide antagonist appears to help prevent the reproduction of the AIDS virus in infected patients whose health has deteriorated during treatment with AZT. Didanosine has been demonstrated to increase the number of CD4 helper white blood cells that are usually depressed in advanced stages of AIDS.*

To every thing there is a season, and a time to every purpose under the heaven:

A time to be born, and a time to die; a time to plant,

and a time to pluck up that which is planted;

A time to kill, and a time to heal; a time to break down, and a time to build up;

A time to weep, and a time to laugh; a time to mourn, and a time to dance;

A time to cast away stones, and a time to gather stones together;

a time to embrace, and a time to refrain from embracing;

A time to get, and a time to lose; a time to keep, and a time to cast away;

A time to rend, a time to sew; a time to keep silence, and a time to speak;

A time to love, and a time to hate; a time of war, and a time of peace.

ECCLESIASTES 3:1-8

Leukemia Blood Cells—*Chronic lymphocytic leukemia results from an increase in circulating levels of white blood cells (lymphocytes, light pink). This causes a reduction in red blood cells (erythrocytes, red) and other blood components. Chronic lymphocytic leukemia may develop slowly over several years with no symptoms, but it can cause enlargement of the liver and spleen, and anemia.*

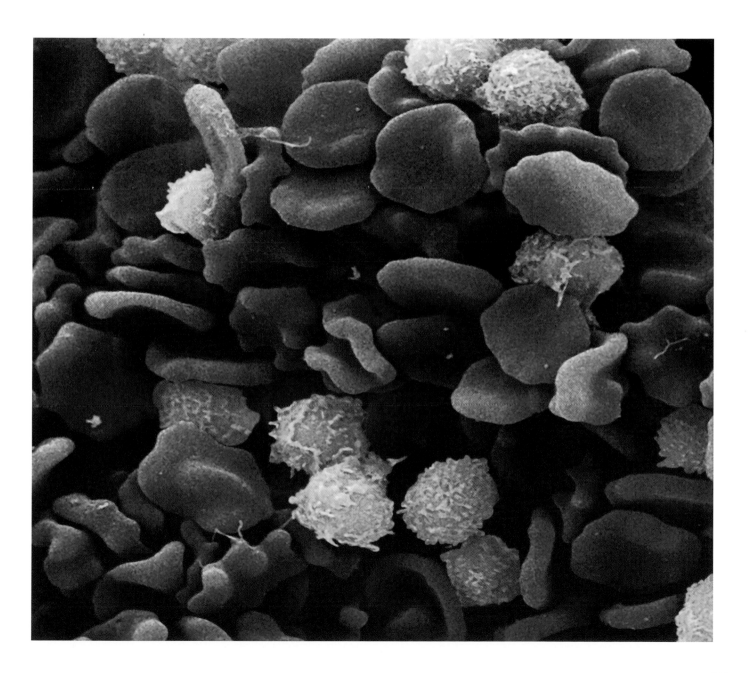

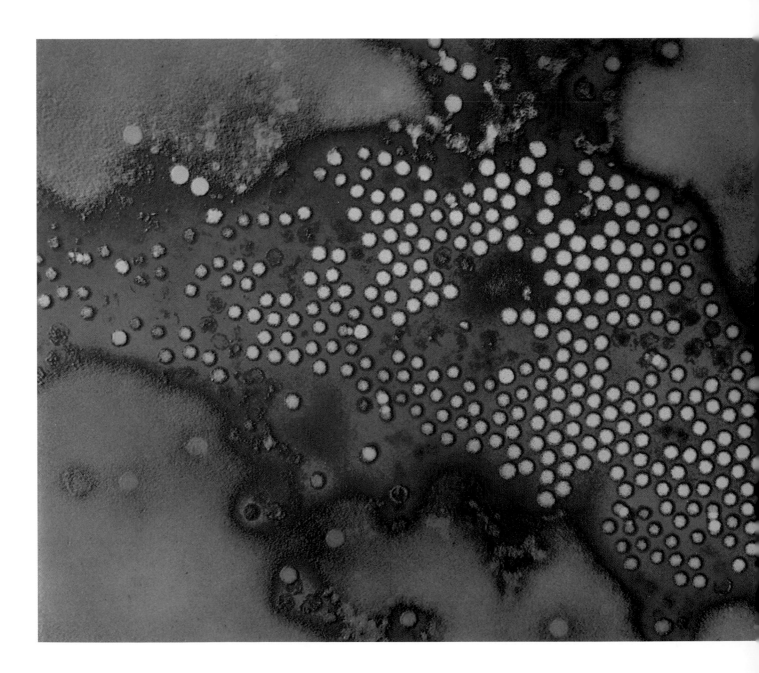

I have had dreams and I have had nightmares, but I have conquered my nightmares because of my dreams.

     JONAS SALK, M.D.
        Developer of polio vaccine

It's a calling, if you like, rather than a job. I do what I feel impelled to do, keep things moving in a positive, creative, constructive way, revealing the truth and beauty that exists in life and in nature.

     JONAS SALK, M.D.

Human Polio Virus—Viral poliomyelitis, *Polio, enters its host via the oral route through contaminated water, food, or saliva and replicates itself in the B- and T-cells in the small intestine. In the absence of a strong immune response, the virus enters the bloodstream and in about 1% of those infected the polio virus attacks the motor neurons and the central nervous system, causing lifelong paralysis or death.*

The essence of life is statistical improbability on a colossal scale.

RICHARD DAWKINS
The Blind Watchmaker

Apoptosis or "Programmed Cell
Death"—*Apoptosis plays an important role in
the homeostasis and development of all tissues within an
organism. In contrast to necrosis (cell death by accident),
apoptosis is a well-regulated physiological process. Any disturbance
of the balance between cell proliferation and cell death maintained by
apoptosis can result in serious disease, in particular, cancer.*

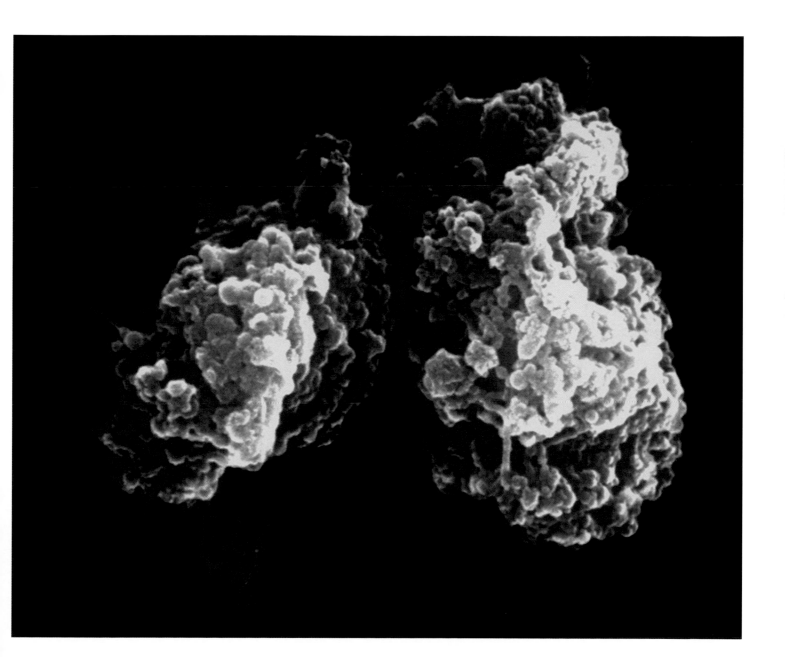

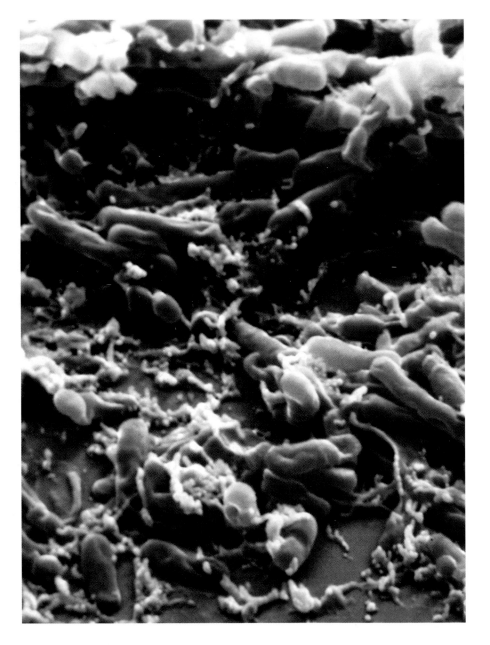

To be a doctor, then, means much more than to dispense pills or to patch up or repair torn flesh and shattered minds. To be a doctor is to be an intermediary between man and God.

FELIX MARTI-IBANEZ
To Be a Doctor

Mycobacterium Tuberculosis *is an acid-resistant, malleable, immobile, red-shaped bacterium. The tuberculosis pathogens travel through fluids to the lung alveoli where they are taken up by macrophages. Macrophages do not dismantle the bacteria. Instead, the bacteria multiply within the macrophages, as tuberculoid granulomas.*

Mites: Scabies, Sarcoptes—*A few mites in the dermis of the skin. The females drill themselves into the skin and advance to the growth layer, which is their subsistence and egg storage region. The infestation is transferred by close body contact.*

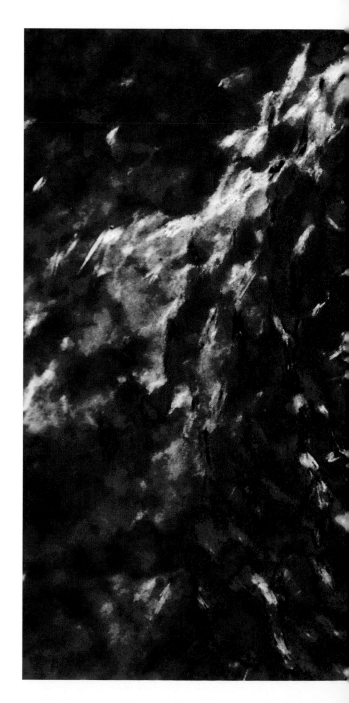

It's supposed to be a professional secret, but I'll tell you anyway. We doctors do nothing. We only help and encourage the doctor within.

⌐ ALBERT SCHWEITZER

Everything on the earth has a purpose, every disease an herb to cure it, and every person a mission. This is the Indian theory of existence.

⌐ MOURNING DOVE
Salish Indian

Gramicidin *is a mixture of three antibacterial polypeptides that work together to form a channel that spans cell membranes. The antibiotic increases the permeability of the bacterial cell membrane to inorganic cations by forming a network of channels through the normal lipid bilayer of the membrane. Medicinally, gramicidin is often used in a combination with other drugs for treating inflammation of the skin, eyes and ears.*

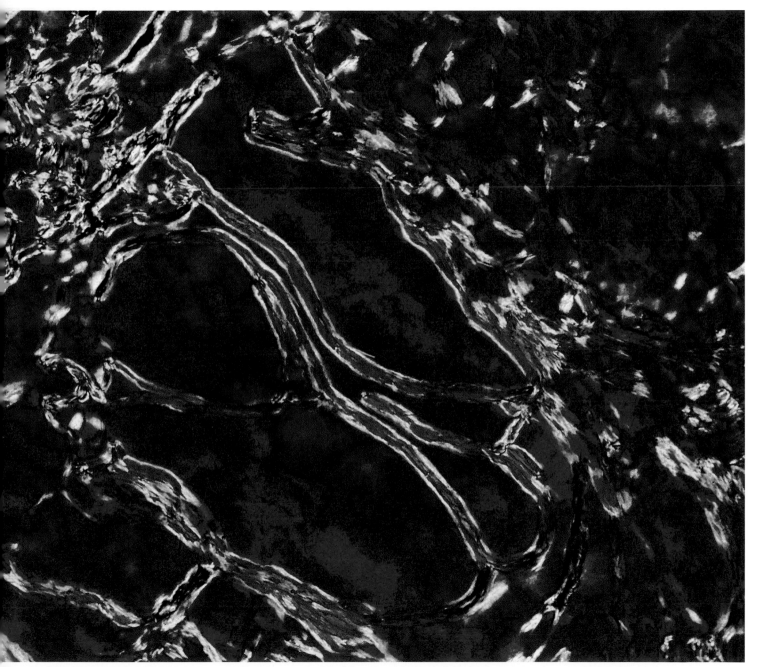

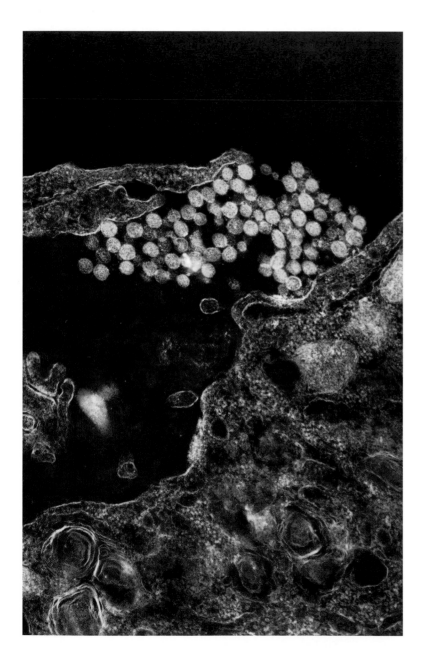

In the final analysis, the questions of why bad things happen to good people transmutes itself into some very different questions, no longer asking why something happened, but asking how we will respond, what we intend to do now that it happened.

    RABBI HAROLD S. KUSHNER
    When Bad Things Happen to Good People

Hantavirus Infection—*Hantavirus particles (yellow/green) can be seen bursting from a human cell. This virus causes hemorrhagic fever with renal syndrome (HFRS) or Hantavirus pulmonary syndrome (HPS). It contains ribonucleic acid (RNA) genetic material that is held inside a protein coat (capsid). Symptoms range from fever and muscle weakness (myalgia) to hemorrhage and cardiovascular instability, which can lead to death.*

A miracle, my friend, is an event which creates faith. That is the purpose and nature of miracles. They may seem very wonderful to the people who witness them, and very simple to those who perform them. That does not matter: if they confirm or create faith they are true miracles.

GEORGE BERNARD SHAW
The Archbishop in *Saint Joan*

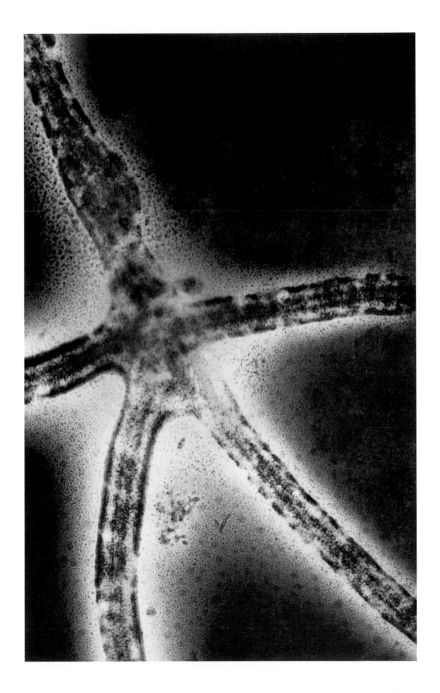

Ebola Virus Replication—*This filovirus, which causes Ebola fever, replicates inside the host's cells, forming a spindle (center left) from which new particles are released. Ebola is contracted by handling material from infected animals, or through contact with the blood or other body fluids of infected patients. It causes a fever, severe hemorrhaging and central nervous system damage. There is no cure, but most victims recover if given excellent supportive therapy.*

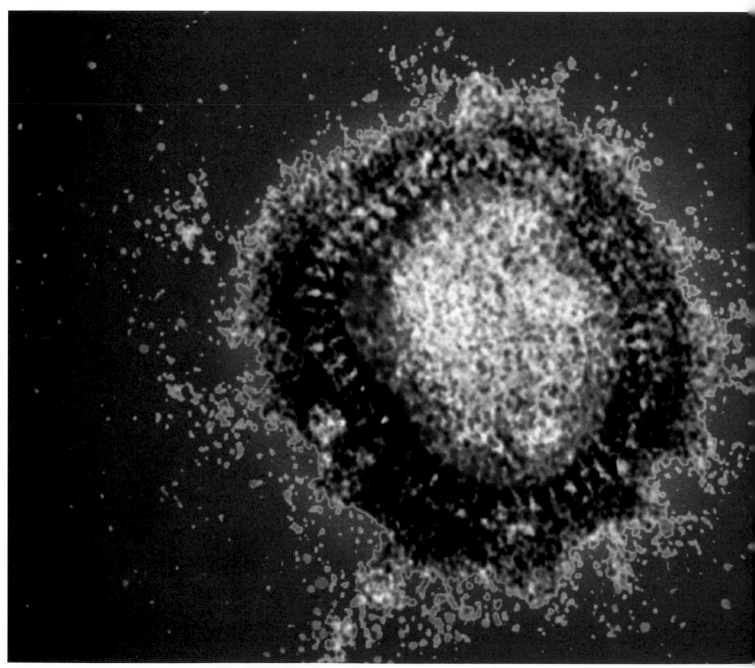

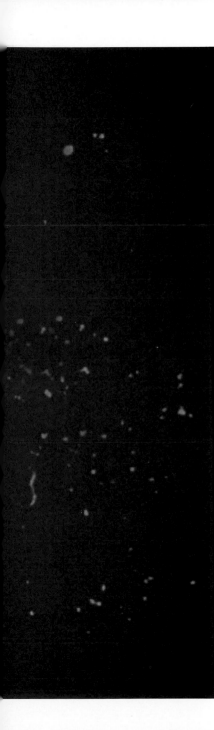

The greatest mystery is not that we have been flung at random between the profusion of matter and of the stars, but that within this prison we can draw from ourselves images powerful enough to deny our nothingness.

ANDRÉ MALRAUX
French man of letters, statesman

✦

Influenza Virus—*Influenza, or
"flu," is an infection of the respiratory tract
that can affect millions of people every year. Influenza
is spread from person to person through mists or sprays of
infectious respiratory secretions caused by coughing and sneezing.
Each year about 20,000 Americans die because of influenza or influen-
za-related pneumonia. Over 90% of the deaths occur in persons aged 65
years and older. A global epidemic, or pandemic, of influenza A in 1918 caused
over 20 million deaths worldwide and 500,000 deaths in the United States.*

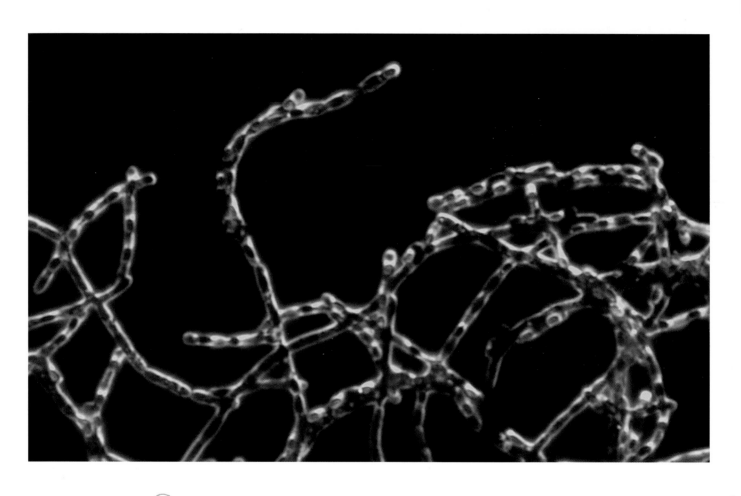

Shall we receive the good at the hand of God, and not receive the bad?

❧ JOB 2:10 ❧

I went through many stages. At times I felt that God was cruel, that God was absent. The main thing I felt was that God was silent. But it's still a question: Was He indifferent? Was He cruel? Was He trying to punish for love? My questioning of God goes on. But even from the beginning I believed in questioning God from inside faith, not from outside faith. It is because I believe that I am all the time questioning.

ELIE WIESEL
Interview with *Bostonia*

Anthrax, Bacillus with Spores—*Anthrax is an acute infectious disease caused by the spore-forming bacterium* Bacillus anthracis. *Anthrax most commonly occurs in wild and domestic lower vertebrates (cattle, sheep, goats, camels, antelopes and other herbivores), but it can also occur in humans when they are exposed to infected animals or tissue from infected animals. Inhalation anthrax is usually fatal, with initial symptoms resembling a common cold. After several days, the symptoms may progress to severe breathing problems and shock. Cutaneous or intestinal anthrax have much lower rates of fatality.*

Yersinia Pestis *is the bacterium which causes bubonic plague (the Black Death of the Middle Ages). Here, two recently divided bacteria are seen still attached. They are rod-shaped, gram-negative, and non-motile bacilli.* Yersinia pestis *is primarily carried by the fleas of rats. Transfer to humans occurs when such fleas feed on human blood. Infection is rapid, causing swollen lymph nodes and leading to septicemia and pulmonary infection. Extensive control measures against rats and their fleas have eliminated plague from Europe, but it occurs in other regions of the world.*

There is no death. Only a change of worlds.

❧ CHIEF SEATTLE
Native American, Chief of Dwamish, Suquamish,
and Allied Indian tribes

Faith is not belief without proof, but trust
without reservation.

❧ ELTON TRUEBLOOD

You can never prove God, you can only find him . . .

❧ KATE DOUGLAS WIGGIN
Author of *Rebecca of Sunnybrook Farm*

Amoxicillin *is a semisynthetic derivative of penicillin and an analog of ampicillin that displays a broad spectrum of antibacterial activity against many gram-positive and gram-negative organisms. The compound is stable in the presence of stomach acids and may be given without regard to meals. Like other members of this class of antibiotics, amoxicillin exerts its biological activity by inhibition of the biosynthesis of bacterial cell wall mucopeptides. Unfortunately, amoxicillin is not resistant to penicillinase, so it is not effective against penicillinase-producing bacteria.*

131

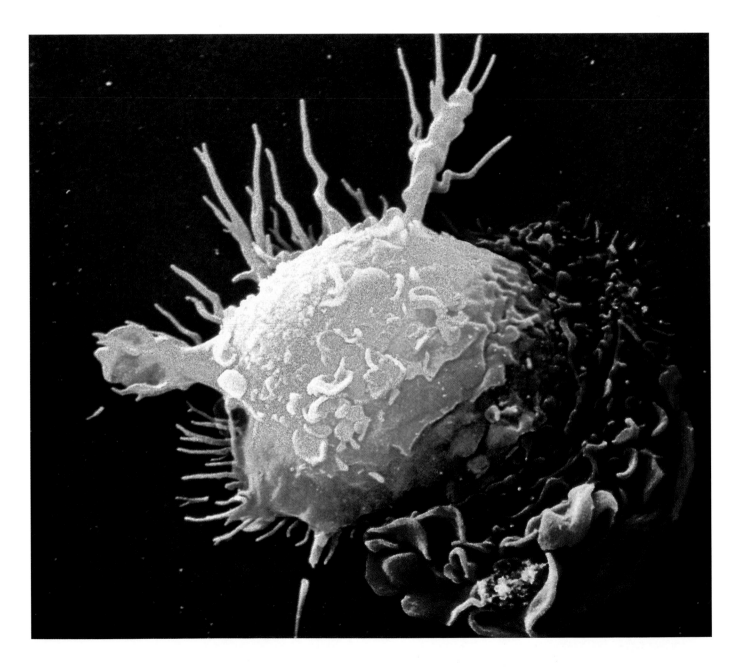

The secret of health for both mind and body is not to mourn for the past, not to worry about the future, or not to anticipate troubles, but to live in the present moment wisely and earnestly.

❧ BUDDHA

If you would be a real seeker after truth, it is necessary that at least once in your life you doubt, as far as possible, all things.

❧ RENÉ DESCARTES

God is not in the vastness of greatness. He is hid in the vastness of smallness. He is not in the general. He is in the particular.

❧ PEARL S. BUCK
Nobel Prize laureate, literature

Macrophage—This macrophage (green) is phagocytizing an invading pathogen. The macrophage is a type of white blood cell, a component of the innate immune system which is capable of engulfing dangerous foreign material. It elongates parts of its cell body in order to surround its target, as seen here. The pathogen is then engulfed, taken into the cytoplasm of the macrophage in a vacuole and digested with enzymes. Macrophages are especially important in removing unwanted bacteria, against which they are the first line of defense.

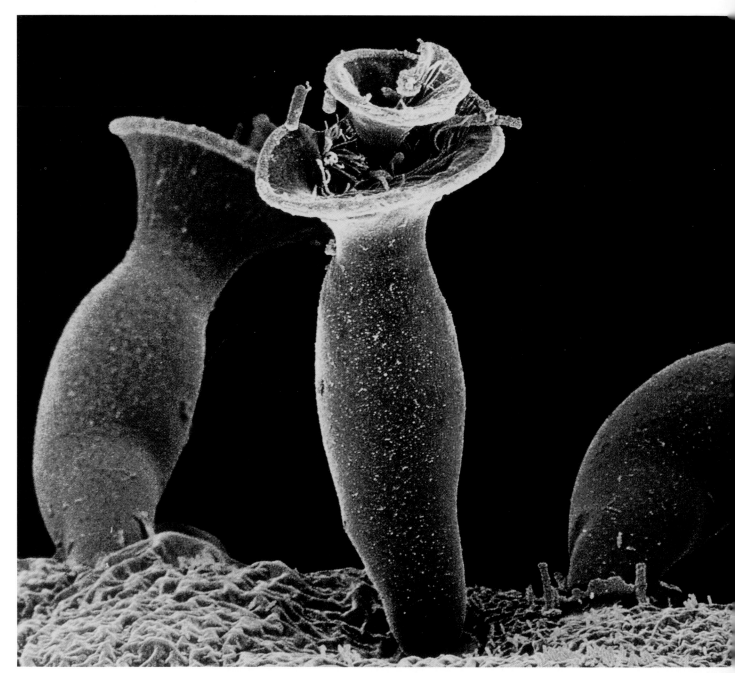

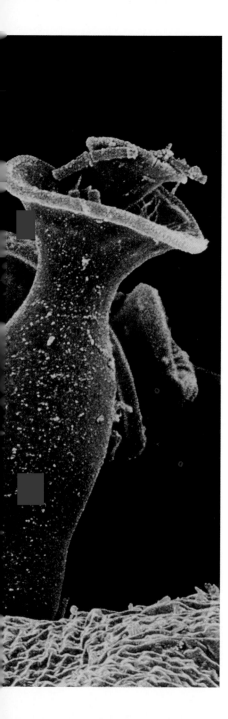

I would rather live my life as if there is a God and die to find out there isn't, than live my life as if there isn't and die to find out there is.

❧   ALBERT CAMUS

In our human foolishness and short-sightedness we imagine divine grace to be finite…. But the moment comes when our eyes are opened and we see and realize that grace is infinite.

❧   ISAK DINESEN

Spirochona Protozoa—*Spirochona gem-mipara protozoa (single-celled animals) are found on the gills of crustaceans when adult, as seen here. Protozoa such as these are being used in biotechnology research at Axiva (part of Aventis) in Frankfurt, Germany. They are being studied to see if they can be used to produce useful biologically active chemicals such as enzymes, antibiotics, and polyunsaturated fatty acids (PUFAs).*

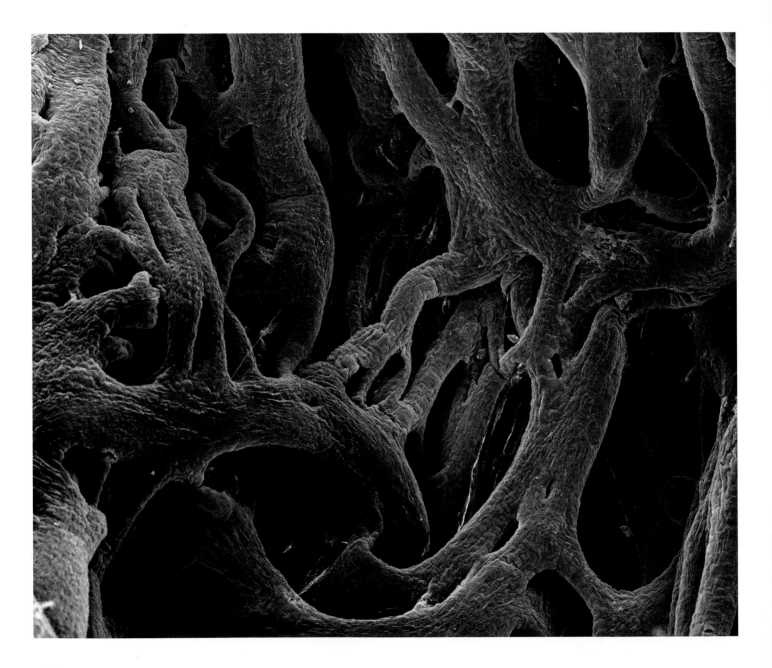

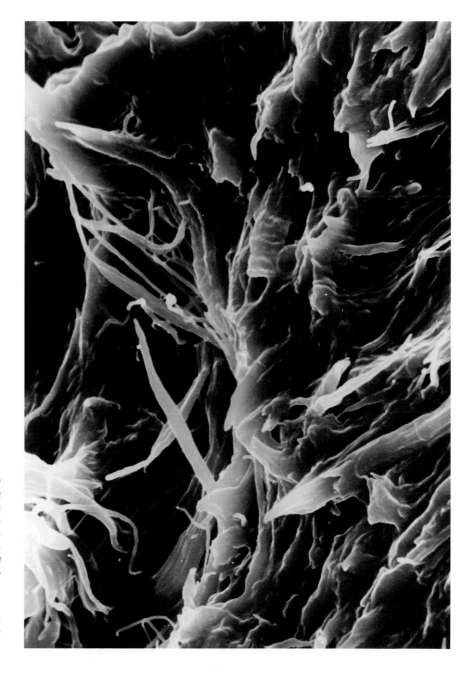

There are only two ways to live your life. One is as though nothing is a miracle. The other is as if everything is.

❡ ALBERT EINSTEIN

Heart Valve Tendons—Chordae tendineae, *tendons which attach the atrioventricular heart valves to their muscles, prevent blood being forced back into the atria (upper heart chambers) from the ventricles (lower heart chambers) during the contraction of the ventricles. The right ventricle (which pumps deoxygenated blood to the lungs) is separated from the right atrium by the tricuspid valve. The left ventricle (which pumps newly oxygenated blood around the body) is separated from the left atrium by the mitral valve. The valves are controlled by papillary muscles.*

Rocket Fuel—*These crystals of solid rocket fuel, also called rocket propellent, are of a double based-type of solid rocket fuel made of a nitrocellulose-type of gunpowder dissolved in nitroglycerine.*

The indivisible is not to be put into compartments. Every fact is a logarithm; one added term ramifies it until it is thoroughly transformed. In the general aspect of things, the great lines of creation take shape and arrange themselves into groups; beneath lies the unfathomable. Which of our methods of measuring could we apply to this eddying mass that is the universe? In the presence of the profundities our sole ability is to dream. Our conception, quickly winded, cannot follow creation, that vast breath.

⌐ VICTOR HUGO
The Toilers of the Sea

Atorvastatin Calcium (Lipitor)—*Lipitor, a cholesterol-reducing agent that helps prevent strokes and heart attack, is classified as a synthetic antihyperlipidemic that acts to lower lipid levels in the body by blocking its ability to synthesize cholesterol. When response to diet and other nondrug measures alone are inadequate to reduce cholesterol levels, lipitor is indicated to lower total and LDH cholesterol levels in primary hypercholesterolemia (types IIa and IIb).*

Faith, then, is like the soul of an experience. It is an inner acknowledgment of the relationship between God and man. Religion, on the other hand, is like the body. It is an outer expression of that inner acknowledgment.

⋈ JOHN POWELL ⋈
A Reason to Live! A Reason to Die!

Faith no doubt moves mountains, but not necessarily to where we want them.

⋈ MASON COOLEY ⋈
City Aphorisms

The spirit is an area of growth most of us set aside, half hoping the day will come when some soul-stretching peak experience will lift us out of our ordinary consciousness for a glimpse of the sacred and eternal.

But we have to prepare our consciousness for taking such a path.

We need to change the way we measure time and to relax our insistence on control.... Instead of focusing on the time running out, it should be a daily exercise ... to mark the moment.

The present never ages. Each moment is like a snowflake, unique, unspoiled, unrepeatable, and can be appreciated in its surprisingness ... if every day is an awakening, you will never grow old. You will just keep growing.

GAIL SHEEHY
Author, lecturer

Embryonic Stem Cells—*These dividing stem cells are from the ventricular zone of the retina of a developing embryo. The ventricular zone is the site of cell division during retinal development. It is the part of the neural retina (left) adjacent to the pigment epithelium layer (right). Dividing cells have bright pink nuclei, while the nuclei of non-dividing cells are blue/pink.*

Dreaming is not just "a long-past period in a time series when the landscape took on its present form and when life filled the void. It is rather the ever-present, unseen, ground of being—of existence."

A. P. ELKIN
Elements of Australian Aboriginal Philosophy

Australian Aborigines (Red Ochre)—*Aborigines often anoint sacred relics with blood or red ochre and fat for use in rituals. The aborigines of Australia believe all living beings, as well as inanimate objects such as wind, rain, and fire, to have a common divine origin. Thus, all things are considered to be a part of one entity.*

Like the reflections of the moon that effortlessly appear in any body of still water, a Buddha's emanations spontaneously appear wherever living beings' minds are capable of perceiving them. Buddhas can emanate in any form whatsoever to help living beings. Sometimes they manifest as Buddhists and sometimes as non-Buddhists. They can manifest as women or men, monarchs or tramps, law-abiding citizens or criminals. They can even manifest as animals, as wind or rain, or as mountains or islands. Unless we are a Buddha ourself we cannot possibly say who or what is an emanation of a Buddha.

GESHE KELSANG GYATSO
Introduction to Buddhism

The mind, the Buddha, living creatures—
these are not three different things.

AVATAMASAKA SUTRA

Buddhism (Lotus Blossom)—*In Buddhist art, a lotus flower is often used to symbolize the Buddha. Buddhism, founded in India by Siddhartha Gautama in approximately the 5th century B.C., prescribes methods of action and thought to reach nirvana, an indescribable release from the self and its desires. After reaching nirvana, Siddhartha Gautama became known as Buddha, or enlightened one.*

We thank you, Almighty God, for the gift of water.
Over it the Holy Spirit moved in the beginning of creation.
Through it you led the children of Israel out of their
bondage in Egypt into the land of promise.
In it your Son Jesus received the baptism of John
and we are buried with Christ in his death.
By it we share in his resurrection.
Through it we are reborn by the Holy Spirit.

BOOK OF COMMON PRAYER

For everything which is visible
is a copy of that which is hidden.

THE TEACHINGS OF SILVANUS
Translated by Malcolm L. Peel
and Jan Zandee

Christianity (Baptismal Water)—Baptismal water is used in the Christian faith. Christianity stems from the life, teachings, death, and resurrection of Jesus of Nazareth, which are narrated in the New Testament of the Bible. Millions of Christians worldwide also re-enact an important episode in Jesus' life, the Last Supper, as a part of worship called Holy Communion or Holy Supper.

All (human) creatures are God's children,
and those dearest to God are those
who treat His children kindly.

❧   ISLAM HADITH OF BAIHAQI   ☙

O man! Verily you are ever toiling on toward
your Lord—painfully toiling—but you shall meet Him…
You shall surely travel from stage to stage.

❧   THE QUR'AN 84.6, 19   ☙

We believe in God, and what has been revealed
to Abraham, Ishmael, Isaac, Jacob, and the Tribes,
and in what was given to Moses, Jesus, and the
Prophets from their Lord. We make no distinction
between any of them, and to God do we submit.

❧   THE QUR'AN 3.84   ☙

*Islam (Rose Water)—Rose water is used in Islamic rituals to cleanse the self prior to prayer. Founded in the 7th
century A.D. by the prophet Muhammad, Islam calls its faithful to maintain a strict adherence to certain religious
practices, including the Salat, formal worship performed five times a day.*

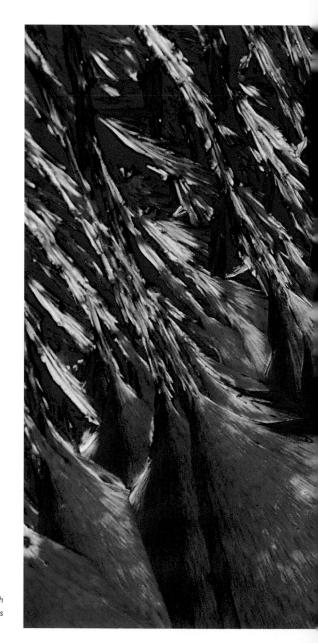

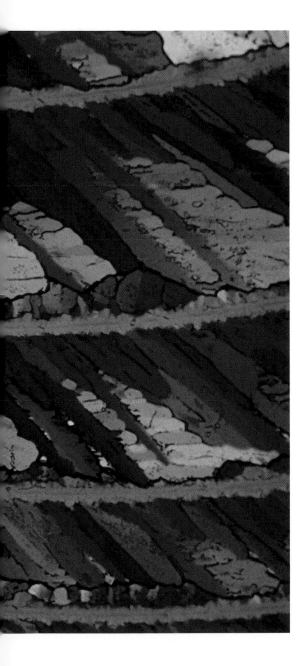

Despise no man and consider nothing impossible,
for there is no man who does not have his hour
and there is no thing that does not have its place.

❧   THE TALMUD   ❧

I the Lord search the mind and try the heart,
to give to every man according to his ways,
according to the fruit of his doings.

❧   JEREMIAH 17:10   ❧

Judaism (Palm Tree)—*Jewish custom provides for the planting of a tree in Israel to commemorate the life of a deceased person. Judaism encompasses a set of beliefs and principles that are applied to all areas of human existence. Daily worship, holidays, and ceremonies marking events in individuals' lives are heavily based on history and tradition.*

Ultimately we cannot call shamans healers. They are only
a reflection of nature principles, which work through them:
through their openness, nature principles flow freely,
because shamans embody freedom from human laws and ideas.
They are the channels through which nature flows through us,
the window into the primal world.

◇   HOLGER KALWEIT   ⋈
Shamans, Healers and Medicine Men

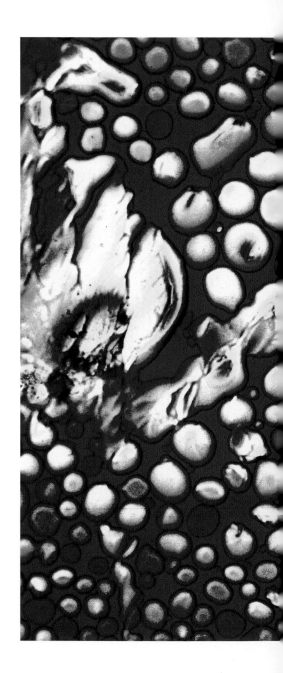

When a man does a piece of work which is admired by all,
we say that it is wonderful; but when we see the changes of day
and night, the sun, the moon, and the stars in the sky, and the
changing seasons upon the earth, with their ripening fruits,
anyone must realize that it is the work of someone
more powerful than man.

◇   CHASED-BY-BEARS   ⋈
Santee-Yanktonai Sioux

Shamanism (Pearl)—*Shamans find a variety of substances useful in performing healing ceremonies, including bone, wood, and pearl, minerals, precious stones, and some metals such as copper. Shamanism is probably the oldest-known form of healing, which is based on the religious belief that all illnesses are derived from an imbalance of spiritual energy. The Shamanists believe that all illnesses can be corrected by shamans (medicine men or women) who can see the spiritual forms of energy and determine whether they are in balance.*

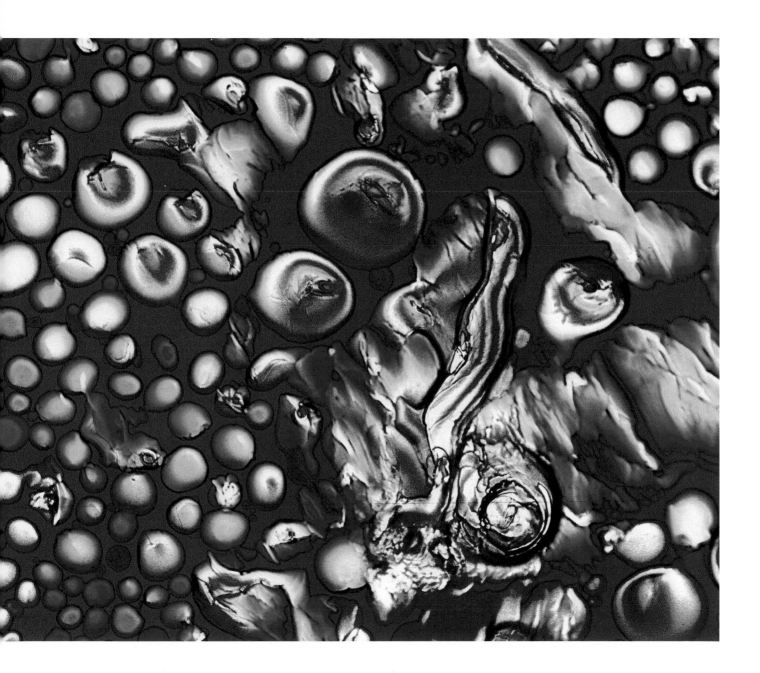

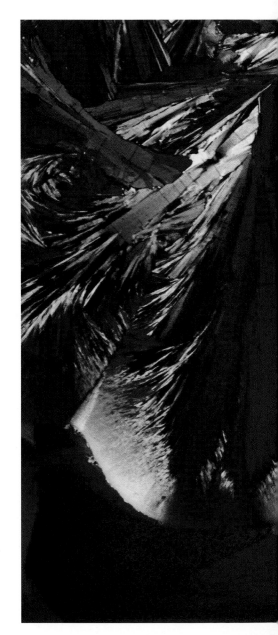

Concealed in the heart of all beings is the Atman,
the Spirit, the Self; smaller than the smallest atom,
greater than the vast spaces.

THE UPANISHADS

Hinduism (Rose Attar)—*Different sects of
the Hindu religion worship deities through household and
temple offerings, such as Rose Attar. Food, flowers, and incense
also are commonly used. Hinduism features at its core a fundamental belief in the incorporation of the self, or Atman, with Brahman,
the infinite, cosmic whole.*

158

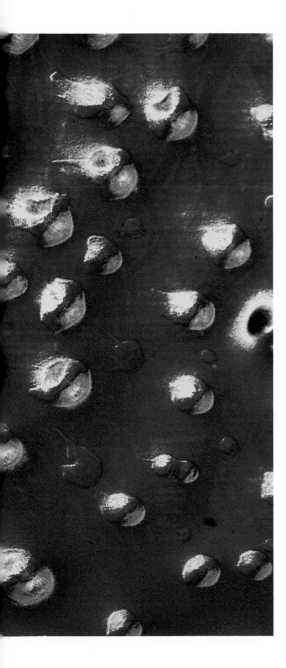

Charity has no label,
compassion no religion,
wisdom no dogma,
empathy no rules.

Integrity needs no laws,
enlightenment no temples.

Living in total harmony with Tao is beyond culture,
oneness with Tao beyond philosophy.

Emptiness and silence cannot be defined.
The Way has no name,
for it is
Tao.

LAO TZU
Tao Te Ching

Taoism (Gold Metal)—*Gold
metal is one of the five parts of the sky in the
Taoist faith: water, fire, wood, metal and earth. The
Taoist religion was founded by Lao Tzu who lived from 604 to
531 B.C. and was a contemporary of Confucius. Taoism was started as a theory of philosophy and psychology, but later developed into a
religion about 440 B.C. when it was adopted as a state religion in China.

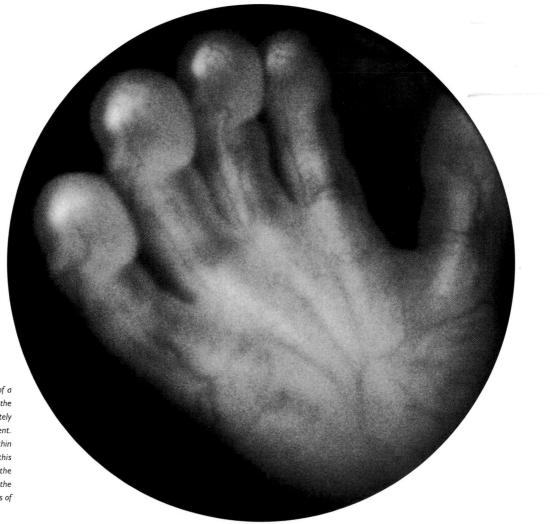

Fetus hand—*Image of a human fetus hand, in the womb, after approximately 3 months of development. The fetal skin is very thin and transparent at this stage, and allows the developing bones of the fingers and blood vessels of the hands to be seen.*

Let your heart guide you. It whispers, so listen closely.

⚛ THE LAND BEFORE TIME ⚛